IMAGES
of America

Cambridge Police Department

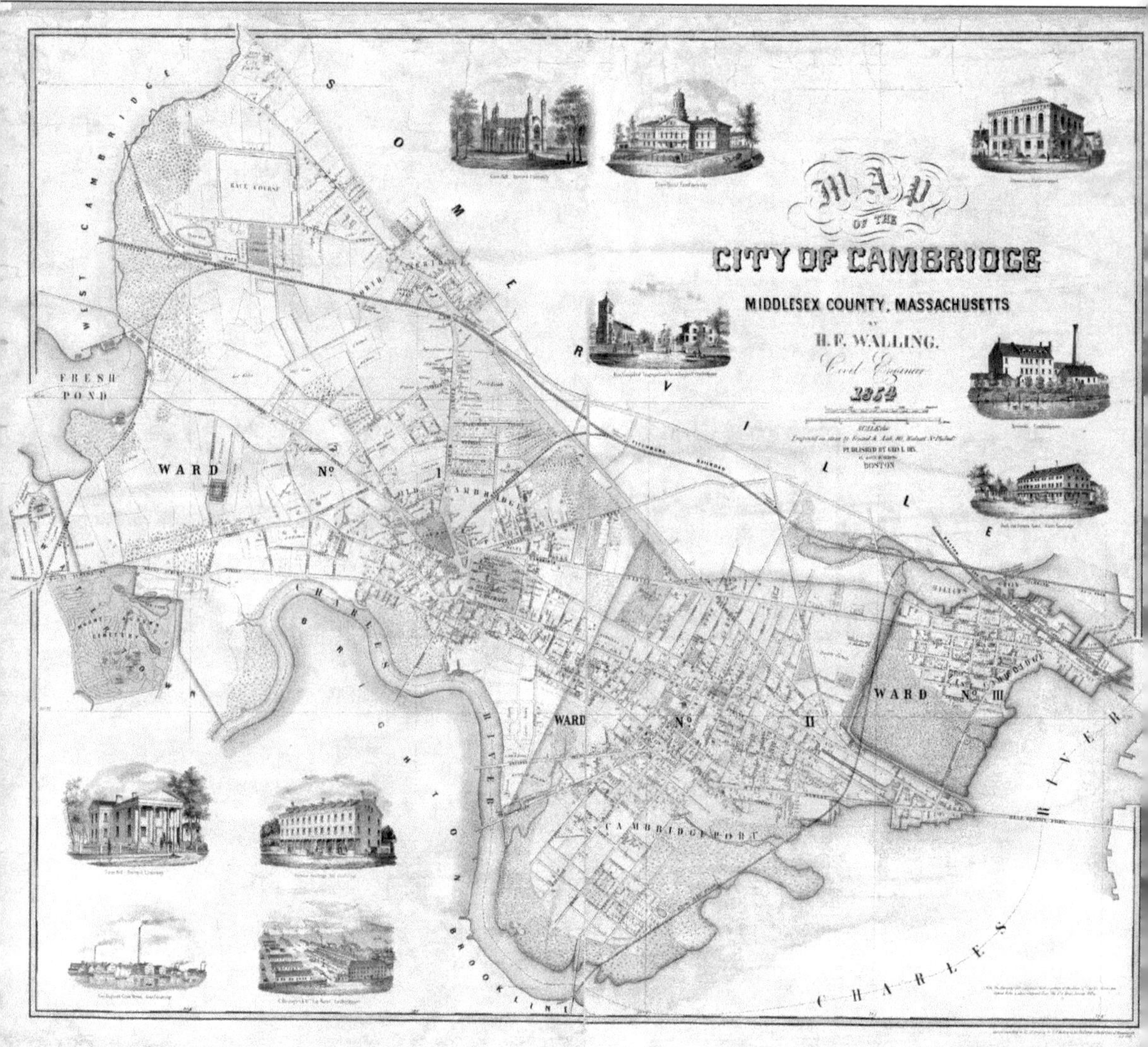

This is a map of Cambridge as it appeared in 1854. It was divided into three wards and controlled by three principal constables. Ward 1 was Old Cambridge, on the left; Cambridgeport was Ward 2 in the middle; and East Cambridge was Ward 3, on the right. The three-constable system was replaced with the official organization of the police department in 1859 and the appointment of John C. Willey as police chief. (Courtesy of Henry Francis Walling, Harvard University.)

On the cover: Officer Carl Sparre is pictured in front of the old Central Square station in October 1960 with eight brand-new Ford police cruisers. This station was in use as police headquarters from 1933 to 2008. Officer Sparre, whose outstanding career spanned over 36 years, retired in 1992. (Courtesy of the Cambridge Police Identification Unit.)

IMAGES
of America

Cambridge Police Department

David J. Degou
Foreword by Commissioner Robert C. Haas

ISBN 978-1-5316-4029-3

Published by Arcadia Publishing
Charleston SC, Chicago IL, Portsmouth NH, San Francisco CA

Library of Congress Control Number: 2008934515

For all general information contact Arcadia Publishing at:
Telephone 843-853-2070
Fax 843-853-0044
E-mail sales@arcadiapublishing.com
For customer service and orders:
Toll-Free 1-888-313-2665

Visit us on the Internet at www.arcadiapublishing.com

*Dedicated to all those who have served the
Cambridge Police Department*

Contents

ACKNOWLEDGMENTS

I wish to thank everyone who submitted photographs and provided information for the project. Without the teamwork, professionalism, and contribution of so many people, this book would never have been possible.

Lillian Gallagher, my administrative assistant, provided hours of research and assistance that were imperative in the completion of this book. Special thanks to the following at the Cambridge Police Department: Commissioner Robert C. Haas, Deputy Steven Williams, Shawn Dolan-Tavares, Sgt. Joseph DeSimone, Brooke Miller, Peter Kunzel, Gregory Trimboli, and Diana Kardashian. Thank you to officer Stephen Bikofsky for his many photograph submissions and insight.

Thank you also to retired captain Joseph Grainger and Leona Grainger for the submission of many photographs and hours of consultation.

I also wish to acknowledge retired captain William Burke, who gave up much of his time to assist me in identifying the people, places, and times found in many of these photographs.

From the Cambridge Historical Commission, thank you to the following: executive director Charles M. Sullivan, Kathleen L. Rawlins, and Sarah Burks. From the Cambridge city clerk's office, thank you to city clerk Margaret D. Drury, Donna Lopez, Mary Beth Cosgrove, and Paula Crane.

From the Cambridge Historical Society, thank you to Mark J. Vassar. From the Boston Public Library's print department and photograph collection, thank you to Aaron Schmidt.

Finally, thank you to my wife, Harriet, for her encouragement throughout the completion of this project.

FOREWORD

Contained within this book is a compilation of pictures that only in part depicts the progress and rich history of the Cambridge Police Department. It is a department that takes its history and traditions seriously.

The Cambridge Police Department has undergone many reformations. It was a department that was confronted with many of the trials and tribulations that many police departments have undergone from the time of their origins through periods of civil unrest, fiscal hardships, segregated housing, and into the era of community-oriented and problem-solving policing. It was a police department that had its own internal strife, as the department grew and reformed over these past decades. What makes the Cambridge Police Department so remarkable is that it has surpassed many of its contemporaries. It is a police department that has taken the concept of community-oriented policing and precepts of problem-solving policing beyond what most would expect to see in an urban environment.

The city of Cambridge is a special place. It enjoys the fame of being the home of two of the most prestigious world-class universities: Harvard University and Massachusetts Institute of Technology. It is the biotech capital of the United States and arguably of the world. It is fast becoming a place where many start-up research and development companies are first establishing themselves so as to take advantage of the intellect and talent that has defined Cambridge. Many of the city's squares such as Harvard Square, Central Square, Porter Square, and Inman Square all possess unique features and histories special to those centers and yet are what makes this city a special social center. It is a city that promotes and celebrates its diversity. It is an urban center in its own right, despite its proximity to Boston. Cambridge is set apart from its neighboring communities in that it has carved out a niche and continues to strive to build on what makes it so unique.

Given the dynamics of the city, there are a great many demands and a higher level of expectation under which the city departments are expected to perform. The members of the police department have taken up this challenge and provide a brand of policing that defies all the precepts of urban policing. The quality of interaction of the police officers and nonsworn staff with the public it serves is truly remarkable. What makes this achievement so remarkable is that the Cambridge Police Department was not unlike so many other urban police departments that had a checkered past. It was a police department that dealt with many insurmountable challenges, and yet due to the pride and caliber of its personnel, the department, like the city it serves, rose to levels that few places are able to achieve.

Presently, the police department is staffed by 277 sworn officers and 37 civilian employees. Many of its members are the sons and daughters of former police officers. There are members of the police department who are the third and fourth generation of Cambridge police officers. It is a department that cherishes its traditions, but also one not recalcitrant in pursuing its future.

It is a department that has leveraged technology as a tool to advance how policing is administered. The department actively uses information to drive its resources. Armed with that information, the department is forecasting where future crimes may take place and situating those resources where it makes measurable differences in reducing crime and disorder. The Cambridge Police Department places a very high value on quality of life issues and engages in a level of partnerships and services seldom seen in other places.

This book represents a glance at our past as well as a jumping-off point for our future. In spite of the old adage, "a picture says a thousand words," it is only part of the story. The Cambridge Police Department cherishes its past, but it is also on the move in terms of taking the art of policing to new heights.

—Robert C. Haas, Police Commissioner

Robert C. Haas was appointed as the Cambridge police commissioner in April 2007. Prior to his appointment as commissioner, he served as the Massachusetts secretary of public safety under Gov. Mitt Romney and as the chief of the Westwood Police Department for 12 years. Commissioner Haas began his policing career in Morris Township, New Jersey, in April 1976. (Photograph by Shawn Dolan-Tavares, Cambridge Police Identification Unit.)

Introduction

Cambridge, settled by 700 English settlers in 1630, is one of very few municipalities in the United States that can trace its history back nearly 400 years. The need for law enforcement was acknowledged and addressed by these first settlers. Appointed by the court on May 9, 1632, constable Edmund Lockwood was the very first law enforcement officer in Cambridge and one of the earliest in the New World. In 1634, James Olmstead became the first constable elected by the townspeople.

As the settlers were Quakers, it is little surprise that one of the earliest recorded actions taken by the selectmen in regard to law enforcement was brought about by religious reason: the apparent decline in church participation. In May 1669, the selectmen issued an order to the constable of the town "upon the complaint of some of the idleness of persons in the time of public worship." The constable was ordered to "look into such persons, that they do attend upon the public worship of God, and God's name and worship not be neglected nor profaned by the evil miscarriages of such persons."

By 1814, Cambridge employed one constable in each of the three principal villages of Old Cambridge, Cambridgeport, and East Cambridge. In 1846, the administration of the police was transferred from the selectmen to the mayor and the aldermen of the city. The entire budget of the department in its first year was $2,017.71. In 1857, Cambridge passed an ordinance establishing the compensation of policemen at $2 per day. In 1859, John C. Willey was appointed the first chief of police.

On June 26, 1860, officer William Loughrey became the first Cambridge police officer killed in the line of duty. He was killed near what is today known as the Longfellow Bridge by James Hurley, who three weeks prior had been released from prison for robbery. Officer Loughrey left behind a wife and four children. On May 13, 2002, his name was included on the National Law Enforcement Memorial in Washington, D.C.

In May 1868, Alderman Bigelow submitted a report recommending the adoption of uniforms for officers. Capt. James E. Murray was appointed to the department on May 18, 1870, and retired on November 1, 1930. Capt. James E. Murray was the longest-serving police officer in the history of the Cambridge Police Department. An officer at the age of 86, he was considered the oldest active police official in the country. During his 60 years on the department, he served for 10 police chiefs and was known throughout the nation as an authority on all police matters. Pensioned at $1,500 per annum, Captain Murray passed away on October 3, 1931, less than a year after his retirement.

In 1872, the city purchased the land at the corner of Western Avenue and Green Street for the erection of a new police station that opened on August 17, 1873, at a cost of $85,000. The cost of furnishings for the new police station was $1,612.05. The year 1874 saw the introduction of five Welch and Anders electromagnetic printing telegraph machines, leading to increased communication between headquarters and officers on the street.

In 1874, a second police station was built at the junction of Brattle and Eliot Streets and was considered the jewel of the city. The department then consisted of a chief, 4 captains, and 55 officers. By 1877, the annual budget had increased to $66,850.85.

In 1878, Frederick W. Hagar was appointed chief of police and detailed officer Charles B. Jones as the first detective. Chief Hagar also instituted rules prohibiting the appointment to the department of anyone under the age of 25 or over the age of 40. He also instituted a mandatory retirement age of 60. He enacted these rules because officers depended only on their strength and endurance to properly police the city and it was vital that they were in prime physical condition.

In 1880, Chief Hagar purchased 10 pistols at a cost of $10. As the force consisted of nearly 60 officers, it remains unclear how the pistols were distributed. There were 163 licenses for the sale of intoxicating liquors issued in 1880, and the city mandated that each was to be inspected by officers twice each week, once during the day and once at night. In 1886, the city voted to better enforce the standing liquor laws and ordered the police department to take appropriate action against illegal distilleries and offending establishments. As there was no liquor squad, it fell upon ordinary officers to conduct raids throughout the day and night.

By 1880, compensation was set at $2.50 per day after three years service. Appointed on April 14, 1884, Frederick Arthur Robinson was the Cambridge Police Department's first African American police officer. On October 13, 1884, Lothrop J. Cloyes was appointed chief of the department. Chief Cloyes visited police headquarters in Boston and New York and found their system of keeping the pictures of "rogues" to be of great assistance. A sum of $150 was added to the budget for the creation of a "Rogues Gallery."

The civil service law went into effect on March 30, 1885. With the exception of the chief, all officers were protected and governed by its regulations. In 1889, the department purchased 76 revolvers at a cost of $532. The department consisted of a chief and 78 officers. That year 92 search warrants were executed and 50 persons were prosecuted relative to the illegal sale of intoxicating liquors.

In 1889, Chief Cloyes recommended the police signal system to Mayor Henry H. Gilmore, who approved the installation of the system. With the introduction of the new system of telephone boxes, instantaneous communication was established between the stations and every patrolman on his route in the city. The system also kept a record of all the movements of all officers while on duty. This signal system remained in use for over 100 years.

In January 1891, in his inaugural address to the city, the Honorable Mayor Alpheus A. Alger discussed what to do with "old and faithful policemen" who had become "worn out" in the service of the city, because the "time is not far distant when many dismissals will be necessary to keep the force composed of live, active, and able bodied men." Many citizens objected to the discharge of patrolmen who had served the city long and faithfully.

In December 1896, an ordinance was passed placing the city's ambulance in the charge of the police department. It responded to 189 accidents and 62 removals of bodies for the overseers of the poor.

In 1897, the office of deputy chief was created. When not filling in for the absent chief, the deputy chief is charged with the operation of the night unit. Early in 1897, on the recommendation of Mayor Alvin F. Sortwell, the city council adopted the provisions of Chapter 314 of the Acts of 1896 establishing a reserve police force for Cambridge. Five reserve officers were appointed to the department.

By 1900, 107 officers were employed by the department. In 1904, the police department was reorganized and Mayor Augustine J. Daly promoted officer Robinson to the rank of sergeant, making him the first African American promoted to that rank. Sergeant Robinson retired after 30 years of service. Upon his death, the *Cambridge Chronicle* wrote, "He was considered an ideal patrolman and superior officer, and his knowledge of police matters ranked him with the leaders."

On December 1, 1908, Chief Frederick B. Pullen detailed an assistant in the inspector's department as a photographer and fingerprint technician. It was the opinion of the International Association of Chiefs of Police that fingerprints, in conjunction with photographs, were the most certain method of identification.

The Department of Public Safety was created on May 20, 1912. Mayor J. Edward Barry appointed Henry J. Cunningham the first commissioner of public safety. With the election of Mayor Wendell Rockwood in 1916, and the adoption of the Plan B form of city charter, the Department of Public Safety was abolished and the control and administration of the police department was vested in the chief of police.

By 1912, the rate of pay for officers was $3 per day. On a cold January morning in 1921, officer Herbert Halliday, an African American officer, was walking his beat about 3:30 a.m. and came upon a house on River Street engulfed in flames. Dashing into the home he discovered seven residents unconscious from the smoke. Due to the heroic action of officer Halliday, all occupants were rescued and survived, including three small children.

In 1921, Chief John J. McBride created a traffic squad under the direction of Capt. Fred M. Ellis. Initially staffed by seven officers, by 1928 there were 36 men assigned to the squad.

Appointed on March 5, 1921, Edith J. Taylor was the Cambridge Police Department's first policewoman. She was given powers of arrest to go with her $1,300 yearly salary. Officer Taylor's duties centered on youth and family services, and she was credited with putting many boys and girls on the right path. After 33 years of service Taylor retired. She trained her successor, Louise Nelson-Darling, as her replacement. In 1951, officer Edith J. Taylor, Frances Marley, and Rev. Harold Taylor (no relation to Edith) cofounded the Big Sister Association of Boston, espousing, "It is better to have a Big Sister or Big Brother looking after a youngster than to have the police doing it."

Before the patrol wagon was used to transport prisoners, friends and family would follow an officer and his prisoner through the streets to the place of detention. Many attempts were made to win the arrestees release, placing the officer's life in grave danger. On August 4, 1930, Allen T. McPherson, a young Cambridge resident, came to the assistance of officer William Anderson, who was making an arrest of a drunk and disorderly person at the corner of Portland and Main Streets. McPherson was attacked by several friends of the arrested individual and was severely injured. He was transported to the hospital where he died of his injuries eight days later. Two Somerville men were later charged with McPherson's murder. In 2008, the Citizen Service Award was renamed the Allen T. McPherson Citizen Service Award during a ceremony held during Police Memorial Week.

In 1932, the contract for the construction of the station at 5 Western Avenue was awarded to Walsh Brothers Construction of Cambridge for the winning bid of $286,929. According to the contract, the building was to be completed within 270 days of signing and, as far a practicable, only Cambridge men were to be employed in the demolishing of the old building. These men were paid at the rate of 50¢ per hour.

In 1935, a revolutionary two-way radio system was installed at headquarters. It was felt at the time that the radio was the most modern and efficient means of combating banditry.

In 1937, under the direction of Chief Timothy F. Leahy, Capt. Thomas J. Stokes established a special crime prevention bureau to reduce juvenile delinquency. He organized a staff to aid and guide juvenile first-time offenders. He often counseled the youths privately in his office and worked out solutions to their problems.

On December 10, 1941, three days after the bombing of Pearl Harbor, Chief Leahy issued general order No. 62, creating an auxiliary emergency police department and detailed Sgt. Stewart F. Cooper as its first supervisor. In August 1942, Sergeant Cooper was granted military leave to enter the U.S. Coast Guard, leaving the auxiliary police department without a director. Attorney Mosier Goldberg, who then held the rank of major in the organization, was appointed director until September 1942, when police lieutenant Charles P. Donelan was assigned to reorganize the auxiliary police department and lead its 340 members. The duty of the auxiliary police department was to "prepare to keep our city safe." Its weekly program included training in first aid, handling and care of firearms, self-defense, handling traffic, and blackout and raid procedures. The first two auxiliary officers recognized by Chief Leahy were Sgt. David H. Lichter and Pvt. John F. Russell for apprehending a suspect breaking into the Lechmere gas station on the evening of June 23, 1942. The suspect was on parole from the Concord Reformatory when apprehended. In general order No. 78, Chief Leahy stated that the auxiliary officers displayed great courage in apprehending the thief in view of the fact that neither officer was armed, save a nightstick.

In January 1943, in the interest of efficiency and economy, all officers were reassigned to the Central Square station (station 2) located at 5 Western Avenue and the other stations closed. Closed were station 3, located in East Cambridge at 34 Fourth Street (present-day Sciarappa Street) and station 4, located at 2101 Massachusetts Avenue.

In 1967, the tactical patrol force was introduced to the department. Its mission was to control riots, an ever-increasing phenomenon in that tumultuous period of American history. The year 1969 brought the formation of the K-9 unit, marking the coupling of peacekeepers and man's best friend.

The year 1974 saw the appointment of the first African American female officers to the department. They were Lorraine Betts, Clara Scott, Yvonne Hall, Jean Murell, and Waneda Ward.

The year 1981 brought a state-of-the-art communication center employing the most modern computers to assist in the apprehension of criminals. The BAPERN System (Boston Area Police Emergency Radio Network) was developed and continues to allow rapid communication with other departments.

In 1991, Perry Anderson was appointed commissioner of police after a nationwide search. He was the first African American to lead the Cambridge Police Department. He implemented the first appointed command staff of four deputy superintendents and two superintendents, birthing the most sweeping and significant changes in the department in over 50 years.

The Cambridge Police Department, now under the leadership of Commissioner Robert C. Haas fields 277 sworn officers, the majority of which are assigned to the patrol division. Others are assigned to the traffic division, public information office, criminal investigation section, community relations, school resource officers, bicycle patrol unit, accident investigation unit, special investigation unit, quality control unit, identification unit, youth/family services unit, warrant apprehension unit, sexual assault unit, homicide unit, dignitary protection unit, FBI bank robbery task force, licensing/hackney division, FBI narcotics task force, court prosecutor's office, crime analysis unit, records unit, off-duty employment office (police details), information technology, and the police academy.

The department fields approximately 50 auxiliary officers and a nonsworn support staff of 37, including a domestic violence liaison and a legal advisor. The department also oversees approximately 50 school crossing guards. The department's budget for fiscal year 2009 is $37,526,700.

On December 8, 2008, the Cambridg Police Department moved from its Central Square location, a home that has served it well for 135 years. The new location of the department is the ultramodern, 100,000-square-foot, $60 million, stat-of-the-art Robert W. Healy Public Safety Facility at 125 Sixth Street. Due to its low environmental impact, including a living roof, active chilled beams, and recycled regional low-emitting materials, it received a LEED (Leadership in Energy and Environmental Design) silver certification. It is an amalgamation of practicality, environmental responsibility, comfort, modernity, and efficiency. The Cambridge Police Department celebrates its formal 150th anniversary in 2009.

All of the royalties from the sale of this book will go to the Cambridge and Somerville Program for Alcoholism and Drug Abuse Rehabilitation (CASPAR), a homeless shelter located at 240 Albany Street in Cambridge.

One

PEOPLE

Officer Francis Gutoski Jr., appointed to the department in 1931, directs traffic on Cambridge Street in East Cambridge in the early 1940s. The small booths that officers used to direct traffic were dangerous, and some officers were struck by motor vehicles, causing the booths to be removed by the late 1960s. Officer Gutoski was promoted to sergeant in 1956. (Courtesy of the Cambridge Police Department.)

Patrolman John McCrehan

Patrolman John McCrehan was appointed to the police department on April 28, 1884, by Mayor James A. Fox and served the citizens of Cambridge for the next 48 years until his death on February 23, 1932. For 35 years, he was assigned to station 4 in North Cambridge and was known by the older residents for his devotion to duty and his kindness to children. (Courtesy of the Cambridge Historical Commission.)

In April 1884, Mayor James Fox nominated Frederick A. Robinson to become the first African American police officer in Cambridge. When the department was reorganized in 1904, Mayor Augustine J. Daly promoted him to the rank of sergeant. Sergeant Robinson worked in Harvard Square until 1914, when he retired with a pension after 30 years of service. As stated in the December 17, 1914, issue of the *Cambridge Chronicle*, "He was considered an ideal patrolman and superior officer, and his knowledge of police matters ranked him with the leaders." (Courtesy of the Cambridge Historical Commission.)

Chief John J. McBride was appointed to the department on April 27, 1887, and served the citizens of Cambridge for the next 47 years. He was made an inspector in 1902, a captain in 1903, and served as police chief from 1918 to 1934. The father of nine children was popular with the officers in the department and highly respected in the community. He passed away in 1951 at the age of 93. (Courtesy of Robin Murphy.)

Officer Frederick Douglas Gardiner was appointed to the department in 1925. On December 11, 1927, with considerable risk to himself, Gardiner saved the life of a Cambridge resident from being trampled by a runaway horse. Chief John J. McBride commended officer Gardiner for this action. (Courtesy of the Kantor family.)

Charles Presho, appointed to the department in 1896, was promoted to the rank of sergeant in 1917 and retired in 1933. For much of his career, Sergeant Presho was the head of the vice squad, and because of the numerous liquor raids that he participated in, he became known as the "Eliot Ness" of the Cambridge Police. (Courtesy of the Bikofsky collection.)

Lt. Charles W. Wyman, who served the department for 39 years, is seen here outside his home at 207 Lexington Avenue around 1900. On July 14, 1917, at 2:45 a.m. Wyman discovered a break on Carlton Street. He entered the building, which was in complete darkness, and single-handedly captured three men who had broken in and were in the act of stealing property and an automobile. Acting chief Patrick F. Murray awarded Wyman with a commendation. (Courtesy of the Bikofsky collection.)

This photograph was taken in 1915. Officer Thomas J. Riley (third row, center) was appointed to the department on March 17, 1913. He was walking his beat on the evening of November 20, 1920, when he came upon a group of drunken and unruly men. One of the men pulled out a revolver and shot officer Riley in the head. He became the second Cambridge police officer to die in the line of duty. The department established the Thomas J. Riley Lifesaving Medal in his honor. His name was also added to the National Law Enforcement Memorial in Washington, D.C. (Courtesy of Barbara Riley-Rideout.)

Patrick F. Dunlea was born on May 24, 1861, in St. John's, New Brunswick. This photograph was taken around 1915. He was appointed to the Cambridge Police Department on April 6, 1898, after being employed as a woodworker. He served on the department until April 12, 1922. (Courtesy of Mrs. Philip F. Dunlea.)

Dennis Wendell O'Brien, the father of 11 children, was appointed to the department in 1912 and retired in 1943 after 31 years of service. In August 1938, Inspector O'Brien, along with Inspector George Selfridge and officers William Anderson and James Wallace, was involved in a wild shoot-out in Cambridge and Brighton after James Sullivan of Dorchester and his partner Harold Ananian of Roxbury robbed a Jordan Marsh payroll truck of $5,500. During the exchange of gunfire, patrolman Lake of the Brighton Police Department was twice wounded in the hands and wrist, and James Sullivan was fatally shot by officer Anderson. (Courtesy of Lynne McGarity-Perry, officer Dennis Wendell O'Brien's granddaughter.)

On April 1, 1915, officer Herbert Halliday became the first African American officer to be hired under civil service. In 1921, officer Halliday rescued seven people, two brothers, Joseph and Nathan Sciaremco, and five members of the Duane family, Raymond, his wife, and three small children, from a burning building located at 303 River Street. All were unconscious from the smoke when he found them and had to be carried from the building. (Courtesy of Sgt. Leon Lashley.)

Officer George D. Buchanan, seen directing traffic in Central Square around 1929, was appointed to the department in 1924. In 1931, officer Buchanan was commended for working diligently with the Somerville Police in the apprehension of three men for the senseless murder of a gas station attendant in that city. Later in 1931, he arrested several men as he watched an armored bank car in Harvard Square, one of which was carrying a loaded .45-caliber automatic pistol. (Courtesy of George D. Buchanan.)

Sgt. Henry Gallagher, seen here in this 1966 photograph, was appointed to the department in 1953 and rose through the ranks, being promoted to lieutenant in 1971 and captain in 1983. Captain Gallagher received eight commendations from various chiefs during his brilliant 38-year police career. As the department's first tactical commander, he was responsible for the creation and training of all volunteers for the tactical patrol force in 1969. A World War II veteran of the navy, Captain Gallagher was a graduate of Northeastern University and the recipient of a one-year fellowship to Harvard Law School in 1971. He was also the longtime commander of the criminal investigation division, and served as the acting police chief before his retirement in 1991. (Courtesy of the Cambridge Police Identification Unit.)

On the evening of August 4, 1930, Allen T. McPherson was walking down Portland Street near Main Street when he observed that officer William Anderson was alone and experiencing some difficulty in arresting an unruly man. Without hesitation or concern for his own safety, McPherson came to the officer's aid. As they struggled to subdue the intoxicated man, two of the man's friends joined the fray. They attacked and severely beat McPherson and then fled the scene. McPherson was taken to the hospital where he succumbed to his injuries eight days later, on the afternoon of August 12, 1930. McPherson left behind a wife, Margaret, a three-year-old daughter, Mary Veronica, and a one-month-old son, Francis. Officer William Anderson, the father of nine children, continued on with a distinguished career, having received several commendations, until his death on May 15, 1945. In 2008, the department established the Allen T. McPherson Citizen Service Award as an expression of gratitude for McPherson's heroism. (Courtesy of Suzanne Little.)

In this 1939 photograph, officer Timothy J. Callahan, recipient of six letters of commendation during his 32-year career, inspects the property on Squires Court in East Cambridge prior to it being demolished. (Courtesy of the Cambridge Police Identification Unit.)

John F. Teehan was appointed to the Cambridge Police Department on March 1, 1929. He served as a detective for many years in the criminal investigation bureau and received five commendations from the chief of police. On July 4, 1943, around 12:30 a.m., a female resident of Cambridge was in her home when a suspect entered through an unlocked screen door and attempted to assault her. When she screamed, the culprit was frightened and escaped. A week later, the same suspect entered another home and inadvertently left his hat behind. When police responded, they recognized the hat as belonging to an individual who lived nearby and were able to make an arrest. Patrolman John F. Teehan, Philip J. Ryan, and John F. Cosgrove were all commended for their investigation into these incidents. (Courtesy of the Cambridge Police Identification Unit.)

Officer John Cahalane, seen here in 1939 posing outside his home at 51 Brookline Street, was born in Ireland on July 7, 1872. In 1911, after serving for several years with the Metropolitan Police, he was appointed to the Cambridge Police Department where he served for the next 31 years. In June 1916, while assigned to Harvard Square's police station 1, the Cambridge City Council commended patrolman Cahalane, along with Lt. William J. Anderson and ladderman Robert J. Buchanan, of Ladder 1, for exceptional work after rescuing four women from a burning dwelling on Flagg Street. (Courtesy of Shawn Dolan-Tavares.)

Officer John J. Grainger is seen here wearing his summer traffic uniform in 1931. He was appointed to the Cambridge Police Department in 1930, promoted to sergeant in 1939, lieutenant in 1949, captain in 1956, chief of police in 1967, and retired in 1968. Throughout his career, Chief Grainger was considered a "cop's cop." (Courtesy of Joseph and Leona Grainger.)

Chief Timothy Leahy, in his office at the old police station at 5 Western Avenue, displays army cartridges found in the basement of a church in 1942. Leahy served the department as chief of police from 1934 until 1946. (Courtesy of Aaron Schmidt, Boston Public Library.)

Officer John H. "Harry" Bagan was appointed to the department on October 11, 1910, and served for the next 34 years before retiring in 1944. He patrolled the same beat in North Cambridge during his entire career. Officer Bagan was an intimate friend of the Roosevelt family and was honored by an invitation to the wedding of James Roosevelt in 1938. Bagan, who passed away in 1952 at the age of 76, also served as president of the United States Fat Man's Club. (Courtesy of the Cambridge Historical Commission.)

Sgt. John Horgan, seen in this 1963 photograph, was appointed to the Cambridge Police Department in 1947, earning his promotion to the rank of sergeant in 1956. During his 32 years of service to the citizens of Cambridge, he was known for his kindness and easy-going manner when dealing with the public. (Courtesy of Mary Horgan.)

Officer Lawrence Gorman, appointed to the department in 1953, observed two men breaking into Symes Restaurant while working in Kendall Square on September 3, 1960. Officer Gorman attempted to apprehend the suspects when an exchange of gunfire took place. Officer Gorman managed to wound one of the suspects, who was captured sometime later. Officer Gorman was mortally wounded in his effort to avert the robbery, making him the fourth Cambridge police officer to be killed in the line of duty. The department subsequently established the Lawrence Gorman Medal of Honor in his memory. (Courtesy of Kate Conway.)

A *Boston Herald* photographer took this photograph of Sgt. William O'Dell on May 14, 1936, one day after he was made famous by tagging Jim the horse in Harvard Square for improper parking. In explaining the unusual tagging incident, O'Dell said the horse's head was sticking too far into the roadway between Dunster and Holyoke Streets, and he called it a clear case of improper parking. Sergeant O'Dell was appointed to the department in 1908, promoted to sergeant in 1926, and lieutenant in 1939. (Courtesy of Aaron Schmidt, Boston Public Library.)

Detective Capt. Alfred Marckini sits behind his desk working the telephones in the Bureau of Criminal Investigation. After being appointed to the department in 1931, he was promoted to sergeant in 1948, lieutenant in 1956, and captain in 1966. During his 41-year police career, various chiefs commended Detective Captain Marckini on eight separate occasions. One such commendation was awarded on January 23, 1957, for solving a series of arsons in the Greater Boston area. One of these arsons involved the burning of a church in Cambridge in 1956, which caused more than $1 million in damage. Detective Captain Marckini retired in 1972. (Courtesy of the Cambridge Police Identification Unit.)

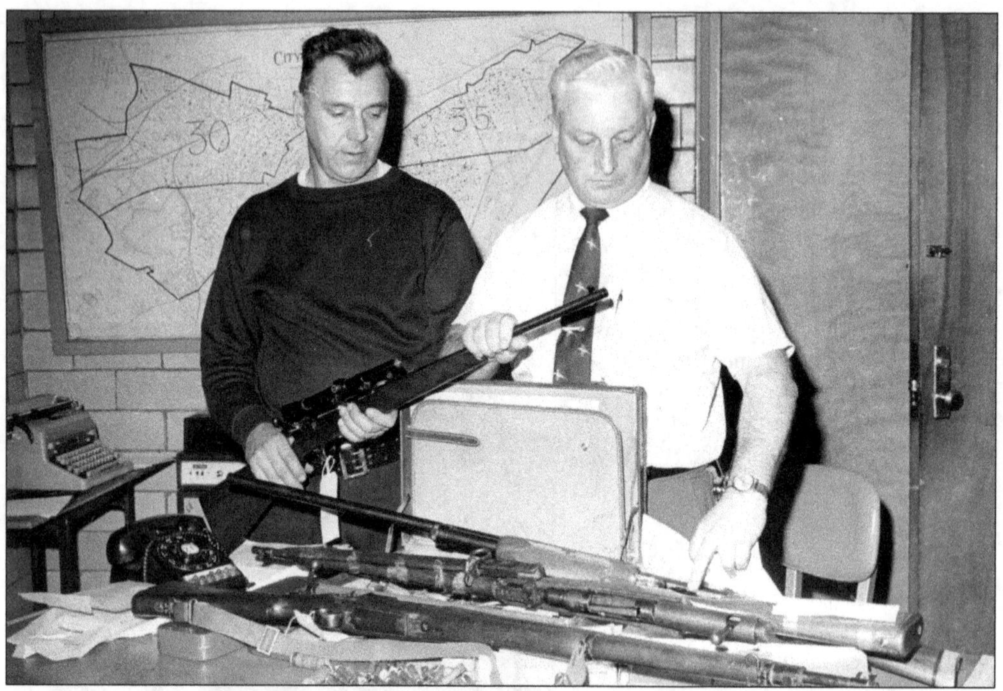

Officer Peter Brusgulis and detective James Roscoe display confiscated weapons taken from a home on Prince Street in 1969 belonging to the Students for a Democratic Society (SDS). (Courtesy of the Cambridge Police Identification Unit.)

In this 1963 photograph, patrolman Robert McManus is seen on his patrol route performing his duty of nightly door checks. That year, walking officers discovered 555 doors that were left unlocked. In 1959, patrolman McManus and his partner, Robert D. Mahoney, were commended for observing five juveniles acting suspiciously and subsequently connecting them to 13 breaks and 31 thefts in Cambridge, Boston, and Somerville. (Courtesy of the Cambridge Police Identification Unit.)

In 1959, police chief Daniel Brennan commended 10 officers, granting them two days off without the loss of pay. Lt. Alfred Marckini and detective John Galligan solved 20 breaks, resulting in three arrests and the recovery of a large amount of property. Detectives Charles Brady, Edward Colleran, and Paul Cloran and Capt. John Grainger recovered $20,000 in bonds, and detective Sgt. John Norton and detectives James Fitzgerald and William Maher arrested five suspects and recovered $26,900 from a theft at the Genoa Packing Company. In all, the Bureau of Criminal Investigations made special investigations of 1,196 cases, resulting in the recovery of $137,206 and the arrest of 892 suspects that year. (Courtesy of Joseph and Leona Grainger.)

In 1962, detective Henry Breen, gun in hand, checks the rear of this building for signs of a crime. Detective Breen subsequently rose through the ranks, being promoted to sergeant in 1966, lieutenant in 1969, and captain in 1975. (Courtesy of the Cambridge Police Identification Unit.)

Detective John Conroy, detective Sgt. Joseph Amoroso, and detective Joseph Miceli display stolen items taken from numerous house breaks on Garfield Street and the surrounding area. An antique clock and several expensive oriental rugs were part of the loot recovered after the arrest of the perpetrators. The breaks occurred in the spring of 1977. This photograph was taken by detective William Durette, crime photographer of the Cambridge Police, in May 1977. (Courtesy of the Cambridge Police Identification Unit.)

Officer William J. Carroll was appointed to the Cambridge Police Department on November 1, 1965. He served as the vice president of the Cambridge Police Patrol Officer's Association and received several commendations during his career. On September 23, 1971, officer Carroll saved a baby's life with the use of mouth-to-mouth resuscitation. In another incident he, along with others, apprehended the individual who robbed the Charlesbank Trust Company in Central Square. On February 4, 1975, officer Carroll passed away suddenly, leaving behind his wife Joan and 11 children. The William J. Carroll Letter of Commendation, presented to deserving officers each year during National Police Week, was established to honor his memory. (Courtesy of Daniel Carroll.)

Patrolman Michael Lombardi (standing at left) with Lt. Chester Hallice (center) and Henry Woods (right) are seen in this 1962 photograph with officers Thomas Mills (seated at left) and John Murphy (seated right). Officer Lombardi, after 23 years on the force, won a special election in 1965 and became a Massachusetts state representative. He remained both a police officer and a state representative for the following six years, being promoted to sergeant in 1967. Lieutenant Hallice was appointed to the department in 1936 and was eventually promoted to captain in 1966. Officer Henry Woods served the department for 37 years and was the 1966–1967 president of the Massachusetts Police Association. (Courtesy of the Cambridge Police Identification Unit.)

Sgt. Thomas Burke performs front desk duty in 1959 at the old Central Square station on Western Avenue. Sergeant Burke was promoted to lieutenant in 1965 and captain in 1969. (Courtesy of the Cambridge Police Identification Unit.)

Alvin Thompson (left) and Vice Mayor Saundra Graham (seated) pose with five African American officers appointed to the Cambridge Police. The class of 1974, from left to right, includes officers Spencer Franklin, Bruce Cromwell, Cecil Wright, James Whitfield, and Lawrence Stead. (Courtesy of Calvin Kantor Sr.)

This photograph, taken in 1977, shows Louise Nelson-Darling displaying her newly received J. Edgar Hoover award. This award was given for exceptional contribution to law enforcement and active community service. She was appointed to the police department in 1950 as the second official female police officer. Chief Leo Davenport stands to the left, presenting her with the award. Lt. Edwin Petersen is to the right. (Courtesy of the Cambridge Police Identification Unit.)

Waneda Ward was appointed on December 16, 1974. She was among five African American female officers appointed to the Cambridge Police Department, all of whom were appointed on that same day. She retired in 2003. (Courtesy of William Burke.)

Speak no evil. Hear no evil. See no evil. Pictured here from left to right are officer Thomas Reid, Sgt. John Walsh, and Lt. Alan Hughes. They are standing at the old front desk before major renovations to the station located at 5 Western Avenue took place in 1978. Officer Thomas Reid was often responsible for some of the humorous and more playful events to be found during front desk duties at the Cambridge Police Department. (Courtesy of William Burke.)

Sgt. Robert Mills, who had many friends throughout the department and the community, is seen here on his last day of work after serving over 32 years in the city of Cambridge. Cambridge Fire Department members present him with a ride in a fire truck and a set of golf clubs as a parting gift. (Courtesy of William Burke.)

In this 1974 photograph, Cambridge police cadets, from left to right, Lester Sullivan, Steven Williams, and Richard Mederos review instruction from a crime prevention arrest book. The three cadets were hired under the Model Cities Program of 1972. Police cadets between the ages of 18 and 23 assisted in any number of administrative capacities throughout the department. (Courtesy of Deputy Steven Williams.)

This photograph was taken in 1986 near Memorial Hall, Harvard University, at the occasion of Harvard's 350th anniversary. On the left, Lt. Calvin Kantor Sr., appointed in 1963, promoted to sergeant in 1975, was the department's first African American to be promoted to the rank of lieutenant in 1983 and in 1992 the first to be promoted to superintendent. Standing to the right of Kantor is Capt. William Burke, appointed to the department in 1960, promoted to sergeant in 1966, lieutenant in 1975, and captain of patrol in 1983. Next to Captain Burke is Captain Carpenter of the Massachusetts District Commission Police. On the right is Sgt. Joseph McSweeney, who after many years in patrol, later commanded the sexual assault unit of the investigations section. (Courtesy of William Burke.)

Pictured here is officer Kathleen Murphy, a 25-year veteran of the department, who was the first female appointed to the rank of sergeant through the civil service process. A lifelong resident of Cambridge, she was featured in a book titled *A Day in the Life of a Police Officer*, published in 1994. She has worked as a patrol officer and detective and has for many years been the commanding officer of the bicycle patrol unit. (Courtesy of the Murphy family.)

This photograph was taken in 1974 at the promotional ceremony of four Cambridge police sergeants to the ranks of lieutenant. On the left is assistant city manager Robert W. Healy, who later became city manger. In 2008, the new public safety facility located at 125 Sixth Street was named in his honor. Second from left is Mayor Walter Sullivan, Chief James Reagan, Lt. Alphaeus Yetman, Lt. Anthony Paolillo, Lt. Edward Stanton, and Lt. Alan Hughes. (Courtesy of the Cambridge Police Identification Unit.)

Officer Frank Pasquarello is the anchor of the longest-running program on Cambridge Community Television. *Crime Time*, as it is known, addresses issues in the city of Cambridge that affect its residents. Crime statistics, traffic issues, and various neighborhood events have all been popular topics on the show. Pasquarello joined the force in 1978 and has become well known throughout Cambridge. Throughout his tenure with the department, he worked as a patrol officer, a narcotics detective, and the first public information officer. (Courtesy of Sarah Brezinsky.)

Perry Anderson, a Vietnam veteran, joined the Miami Police Department in 1969 and rose through the ranks from sergeant, lieutenant, major, deputy chief, and assistant chief. He retired as chief of the Miami Police Department on April 30, 1991. In May 1991, Perry Anderson began a new phase of his police career by becoming the first African American head of the Cambridge Police Department when he was appointed as the first police commissioner. During his tenure as police commissioner he oversaw the most sweeping changes to the department in over 50 years. He implemented the first appointed command staff of the department, which included the first female commanding officer. Perry Anderson was also responsible for the creation of community-oriented policing in the city, a philosophy that is still utilized to this day. These, and many other progressive changes, were the hallmarks of his administration and formed the foundation of future progress beyond his retirement from the department in December 1995. (Courtesy of Giro Studio.)

In August 1996, Ronnie Watson joined the Cambridge Police Department as its second police commissioner, after completing a 33-year career with the Chicago Police Department. In 1963, he was appointed one of the first 63 police cadets by Superintendent of Police O. W. Wilson and subsequently rose through the ranks serving as the commanding officer of various units, including the gambling unit, the organized crime division, the training academy, and the Englewood 7th Police District. His last assignment with the Chicago Police was that of deputy chief of patrol, where he oversaw the activities of five police districts. Immediately upon joining the Cambridge Police Department, he formalized the philosophy of community policing through the establishment of the Neighborhood Sergeants Program, where a designated sergeant is assigned as a liaison to each of the city's 13 neighborhoods to become the focal point of the community's interaction with the department. Serious crime in Cambridge steadily decreased during Commissioner Watson's 10-year tenure, and in his last full year as commissioner in 2006, the city recorded its lowest uniform crime reporting index number to the FBI in over 45 years. (Courtesy of Giro Studio.)

Two

SPECIALIZED UNITS

Members of the traffic squad pose in front of the old Central Square headquarters around 1939. Standing on the far right is Capt. Joseph Kelley, and standing in the foreground is city councilor Michael Sullivan. With their motorcycles are officer Andrew Trodden, Lt. Arthur Fitzmaurice, officer Francis Gutoski, officer James Delaney, and officer John Finnegan. (Courtesy of Dorothy O'Connor.)

Members of the traffic squad Andrew Trodden (left) and Francis Gutoski (right) stand in front of their squad car in 1939. Andrew Trodden was promoted to the rank of sergeant on August 1, 1939. He resigned in 1943 and later became a lieutenant detective with the state police. While a police officer, he attended Boston College, receiving his law degree. In 1959, he was elected to the Cambridge City Council. Officer Gutoski was appointed to the department in 1931 and was promoted to the rank of sergeant in November 1956. (Courtesy of Dorothy O'Connor.)

Pictured in this 1944 photograph are members of the traffic unit (from left to right) Leo Gutoski, Robert Burns, Francis Burns, Francis Gutoski, and Capt. Joseph Kelley. At the time the photograph was taken, the traffic unit consisted of only a captain and 17 men, and its goal was to strengthen the unit after World War II, when more members of the department would return home from overseas. An increase in retail businesses on Massachusetts Avenue and Cambridge Street, as well as the growing population of schoolchildren and college students, all contributed to traffic concerns. (Courtesy of Deputy Robert Ames.)

In the early 1970s, members of the Cambridge Police Traffic Unit are seen at the city's water department, practicing maneuvering around the traffic cones without losing control of their motorcycles or knocking over the cones. The department has conducted and improved many of these trainings over the years. Today motorcycle officers attend a two-week police motorcycle operator course with the North Carolina Highway Patrol. In August 2005, the department replaced the entire fleet of Harley-Davidson motorcycles with new BMWs. (Courtesy of the Cambridge Police Identification Unit.)

In 1949, due to the increasing number of motor vehicle accidents, the traffic unit was staffed with 38 officers. Despite the intense efforts of this unit, there were 1,973 accidents in which there were 7 fatalities and 1,370 injured that year. Several members of that traffic squad are seen here in front of the Central Square station. (Courtesy of Kate Conway.)

Policeman Robert A. Burns, appointed to the department on February 28, 1928, was assigned to the traffic squad and is seen in this late-1930s photograph riding his Indian motorcycle. On June 26, 1941, while working a speed trap on River Street with his partner Malcolm Hillis, they observed an automobile traveling in excess of 50 miles per hour down River Street. Both officers, suspecting that something was wrong, chased the car through Central Square and into the adjoining city of Somerville, where the operator jumped from the car and ran. There was an exchange of gunfire and the suspect, a 22 year old from the city of Charlestown with a long criminal record, was arrested. The car was stolen from the neighboring town of Brookline, although at the time neither officer was aware of it. Chief Timothy Leahy recognized both officers for their power of observation and good police work, awarding them one day off without loss of pay. (Courtesy of Deputy Robert Ames.)

Members of the motorcycle squad, (from left to right) officers Andrew Trodden, unidentified, and Robert Burns, pose for this picture in the late 1930s. (Courtesy of the Bikofsky collection.)

Motorcycle officers Francis "Buster" Burns (left) and Francis H. Gutoski are imposing figures in Harvard Square in the late 1940s. (Courtesy of Deputy Robert Ames.)

Motor officer Salvatore Fusco poses for a photograph with his Harley-Davidson police motorcycle. He is standing outside the old police station in Central Square some time in the mid-1980s. He was appointed to the department in 1964. (Courtesy of the Cambridge Police Identification Unit.)

Members of the tactical patrol force are in the ready position prior to their deployment to Harvard Square to quell the antiwar riot in 1970. (Courtesy of the Cambridge Police Department.)

Officer Harold F. Murphy Jr., a former marine, displays the new tactical patrol uniform in 1971. Officer Murphy continued on with a spectacular 37-year career, rising through the ranks, being promoted to sergeant in 1975, lieutenant in 1983, deputy superintendent in 1992, and superintendent in 1993. In addition, superintendent Murphy is a graduate of the FBI's National Academy. (Courtesy of the Cambridge Police Identification Unit.)

In this 1984 photograph, members of the tactical patrol force pause while providing security for a soccer event at Harvard Stadium. From left to right are (first row) officer Stephen Kervick, Joseph Musto, Aurelio Ferreira, Larry Clarke, Sgt. Richard Bongiorno, and Lt. Donald Carney; (second row) James DeFrancesco, Leonard DiPietro, Sgt. Timothy McCusker, Michael McMahon, John White, Robert Pasco, Lester Sullivan, and Edward Burke. (Courtesy of Edward Burke.)

Members of the SWAT team, standing outside of the Dante Alighieri Society, pose in the ready position in preparation for the 1982 visit of the Italian premier. From left to right are officer Edward Loder, officer Joseph Savioli, Chief Anthony Paolillo, city manager Robert W. Healy, officer Robert Ames, Lt. Donald Carney, and officers Joseph Cozza, Joseph McCarthy, and Frederic Pierce. (Courtesy of officer Frank Pasquarello.)

Executing a search warrant, detectives and members of the Cambridge Police SWAT Team conduct a raid on a house for illegal firearms in 1989. Pictured on the bottom left is Gerald Baptiste. Standing on the left is Paul Burke. Lester Sullivan is utilizing the battering ram to gain entry into the home. Edward Burke is holding the riot shield. Behind him are James DeFrancesco on the left and Anthony Grassi on the right. (Courtesy of Calvin Kantor Jr.)

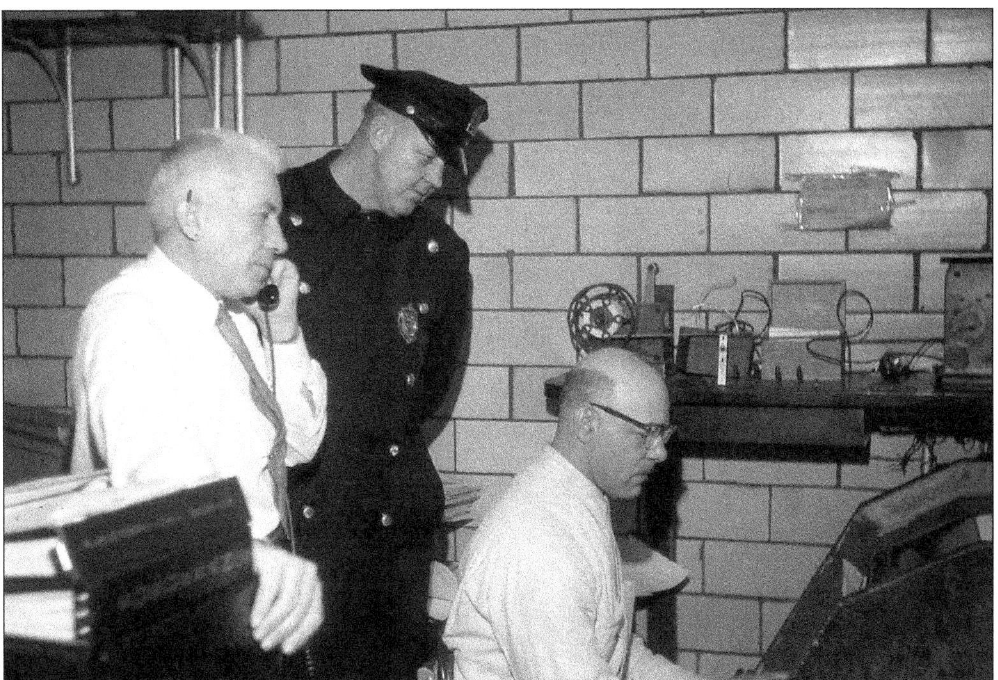
Standing on the left with the telephone is detective William Durette. Officers Francis Seybolt, in uniform, and John Freeman check files for fingerprints in the identification unit in 1962. (Courtesy of the Cambridge Police Identification Unit.)

Richard Sevieri was hired in 1979 as a crime analyst after working for the Boston Police Department. He is considered the father of the crime analysis unit at the Cambridge Police Department and has been instrumental in developing the unit into the significant role it plays today. He has been consulted by many police departments across the country for his wide knowledge of crime and crime patterns. (Courtesy of William Burke.)

Elizabeth Ryan, seen here at the switchboard with her usual smile, was the department's telephone operator from 1943 to 1971. (Courtesy of William Burke.)

While on duty in 1968, canine Sabin could always be counted on to remain "on top of things," including this police cruiser. (Courtesy of Deputy Chief Paul Upton.)

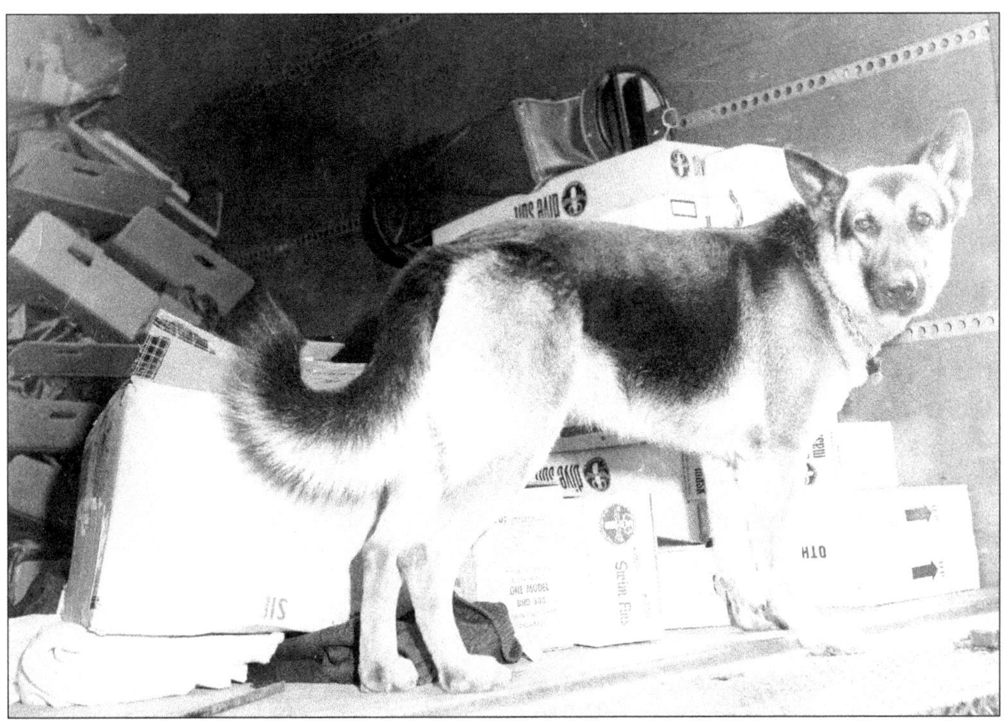

Canine champion Sabin guards $40,000 worth of stolen loot after apprehending a suspect in this 1968 photograph. (Courtesy of the Cambridge Police Identification Unit.)

Canine Barron takes a break from serving and protecting the city in this 1968 photograph. (Courtesy of Deputy Chief Paul Upton.)

Officer Frederick D. D. O'Connor (left) and officer Paul White (right) hold the reins of their canine partners. In this photograph, Major (right) looks particularly upset and his displeasure is clearly visible. (Courtesy of the Cambridge Police Identification Unit.)

Mayor Walter L. Sullivan proclaimed the week of May 25–31, 1969, as K-9 Week in Cambridge. Above, Mayor Sullivan relaxes with members of the K-9 corps and their trainers. From left to right are patrolman John Mearn and Barron, patrolman Edward MacAskill and Champ, Mayor Sullivan, Fritz and patrolman William Cummings, patrolman Frederick D. D. O'Connor and Sabin, and Barron and patrolman Arthur L. Yetman. (Courtesy of Edward Pacheco.)

Officer Paul White with his canine partner Major (left) and officer Frederick D. D. O'Connor with his canine partner Sabin (right) proudly display the trophies they won in various competitions. Sabin was both a state and national champion in 1972. (Courtesy of the Cambridge Police Identification Unit.)

Adam, a valued member of the Cambridge Police K-9 Unit, takes a break for this 1974 photo shoot. (Courtesy of the Cambridge Police Identification Unit.)

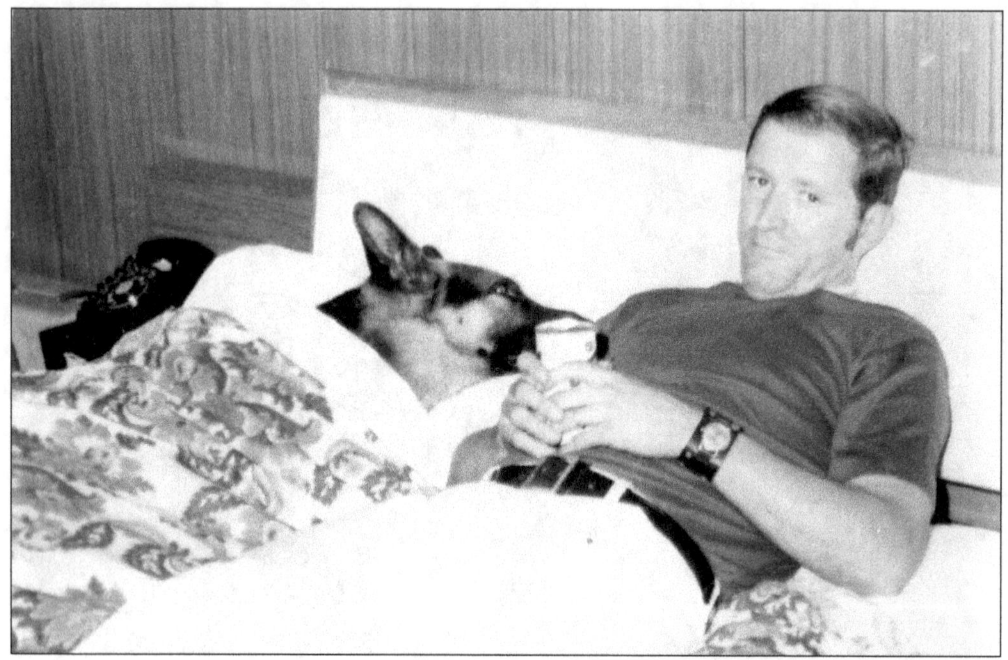
K-9 officer Paul White of the Cambridge Police Department and his partner, Major, take a moment to relax prior to the next day's grueling state competition. The competition, which was held in 1972, included skills such as obedience, article search, attack work, agility, and box searches. (Courtesy of the Cambridge Police Identification Unit.)

Chief Leo Davenport (left) congratulates officer Thomas Tosi (right) and his canine partner Bruin for their second-place performance in the Region 4 trials in Plymouth. In 1977, Bruin also earned the distinction of placing eighth in the nation at the trials held in Peabody. (Courtesy of the Cambridge Police Identification Unit.)

Officer Edward Burke rides his horse, Radar, during Police Appreciation Week in May 1992. There had been plans to establish a mounted unit at the Cambridge Police Department; however, due to budgetary constraints, the unit never materialized. (Courtesy of Cathleen Crowley, Boston Police.)

This photograph of the Cambridge Auxiliary Police Force, with Chief Patrick Ready, was taken in 1952 on the steps of the Widner Library at Harvard University. At that time there were 350 members under the direction of Lt. Daniel Brennan. In 1951, Dr. Walter L. Cronin, director of civil defense, thanked the auxiliary police for collecting $4,727.29 for the Jimmy Fund. That same year, they were fully equipped with uniforms, badges, and nightsticks at the department's expense. (Courtesy of the Cambridge Police Identification Unit.)

Seen here are Cambridge Auxiliary Police who completed an eight-hour radiological monitoring course in 1964 and were assigned as monitors by civil defense director Charles F. Donohoe. (Courtesy of Elizabeth Cahill-Halloran.)

Capt. John Martin, a 30-year veteran of the Cambridge Auxiliary Police, provides direction to those auxiliary officers under his command in this early-1970s photograph. (Courtesy of the Cambridge Police Identification Unit.)

Sgt. Patrick Corcoran (at the podium) and members of the auxiliary police attend roll call in the guardroom of the old Central Square station in the early 1970s. (Courtesy of the Cambridge Police Identification Unit.)

Sgt. Elizabeth Robinson (right) takes attendance and provides some instructions to female auxiliary officers in guardroom at the Central Square station. These auxiliary officers patrolled all public schools and the elderly housing units for vandalism. From left to right are an unidentified officer, Margaret Bolduc, an unidentified officer, and Jeannie Black. (Courtesy of the Cambridge Police Identification Unit.)

In this 1982 photograph, members of the auxiliary police command staff stand in front of a sign posted in front of city hall from Mayor Alfred E. Vellucci thanking them for their service. From left to right are Diamond Vergato, Capt. Patrick Corcoran, Patrick Power, Paul McCauley, Oliver Cox, Vernon Holford, Thomas Poleet, John Martin, Howard Stone, Charles Ames, Henry Lauziere, and Bernie Hill. (Courtesy of auxiliary police deputy Henry Lauziere.)

In the early 1980s, Capt. Vernon Holford (left) and Capt. John Martin (to his left) give instruction to (from left to right in front of cruiser) Sgt. Elizabeth Robinson, an unidentified officer, and officer Donald Langstrom prior to going out on patrol. The members of the Cambridge Police Auxiliary have continuously provided service to the city of Cambridge since 1941, assisting with traffic control at various events. Today they meet every other Wednesday night from September through June. At these meetings the auxiliary are trained in such skills as the use of O.C. spray, Massachusetts general laws, and the concepts of community policing. Vernon Holford, currently a deputy superintendent, has served in the auxiliary for over 55 years. (Courtesy of the Cambridge Police Identification Unit.)

In this 1986 photograph Mayor Walter L. Sullivan presents the Cambridge Auxiliary Police with a new vehicle. This vehicle would be used every night for a four-hour two-officer patrol near public schools and elderly housing units, checking for disturbances, vandalism, and other public nuisance crimes. Pictured from left to right are auxiliary captains Howard Stone and Vernon Holford and Cambridge police captain Patrick Corcoran. Receiving the keys from the mayor is auxiliary lieutenant Elizabeth Robinson. On the far right is police chief Anthony Paolillo. (Courtesy of the Cambridge Chronicle.)

Three

Tools of the Trade

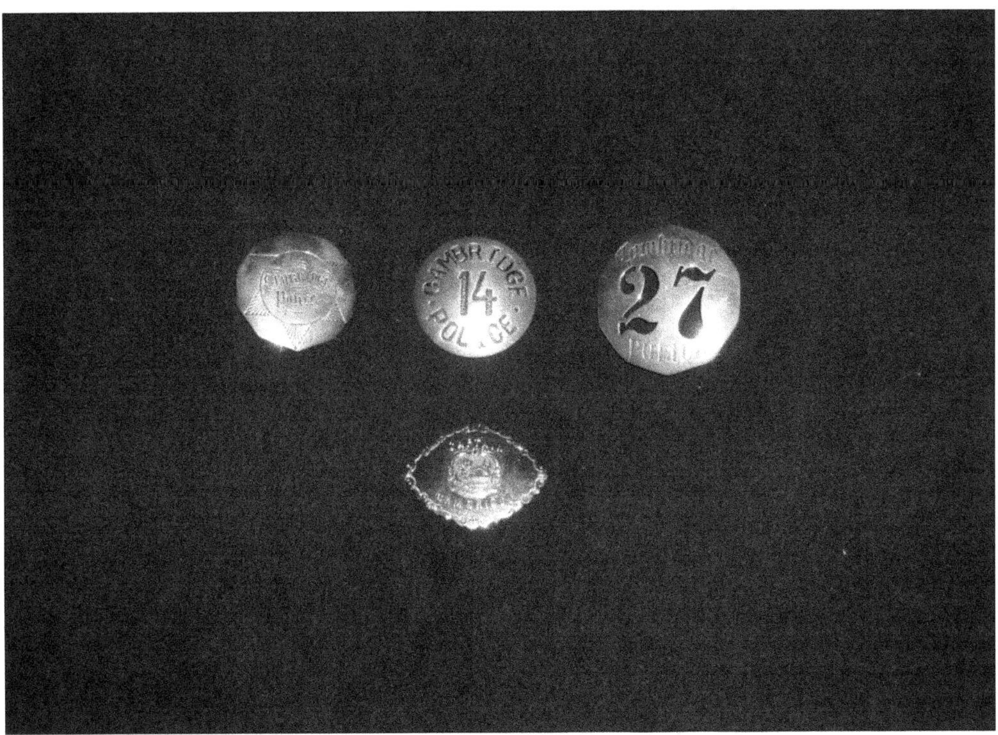

Officer Benjamin F. Higgins, appointed to the department on June 22, 1879, wore badge number 14 (center). It is unknown who the badge on the left belonged to; however, this type of badge would have been typically worn by a superior officer. Officer Charles J. McCann, appointed on May 21, 1889, wore badge number 27 (right). These three particular styles of badges were in use by the department from 1880 to 1909. The gold badge below is a special commemorative badge that was presented to Capt. James Emmett Murray upon his retirement after 60 years of service. (Courtesy of the Bikofsky collection.)

This helmet belonged to officer Michael Culhane, who was appointed as a patrolman on February 14, 1888. This style of hat was worn in the summertime and was made of a lighter material to help keep the heat off officers' heads. (Courtesy of the Bikofsky collection.)

This is one of the Gamewell Company's police telephone boxes that were installed throughout the city during the 1890s. Officers used these boxes as a means of communication to stay in touch with headquarters. At the time, officers would have to bring apprehended suspects to the nearest box in order to alert headquarters that they had a prisoner. A patrol wagon would then be sent to the current location of the officer and his prisoner. Box 34 was located on Sidney Street at the corner of Allston Street. These boxes remained in place until the final box was disconnected in Harvard Square early in the 1990s. (Courtesy of the Bikofsky collection.)

The Cambridge police badge pictured on the left belonged to Lt. Charles Wyman. This style of badge was used from 1920 until 1935 and was worn on the officers' hats. The radiator-style badge pictured on the right was worn on the breasts of the officers' uniforms until 1929. (Courtesy of the Cambridge Historical Commission/Bikofsky collection.)

This police rattle was used as a tool for calling for help when the officer needed assistance. The rattles made a very loud and distinctive sound that could be heard up to 500 yards away. Members of the Cambridge Police Department carried this tool until the mid-1880s, when officers were issued their first police whistles. (Courtesy of the Bikofsky collection.)

This photograph shows the prisoner cells at the old police lock-up at 5 Western Avenue. These cells were in use for 75 years from 1933 to 2008. (Courtesy of the Cambridge Police Identification Unit.)

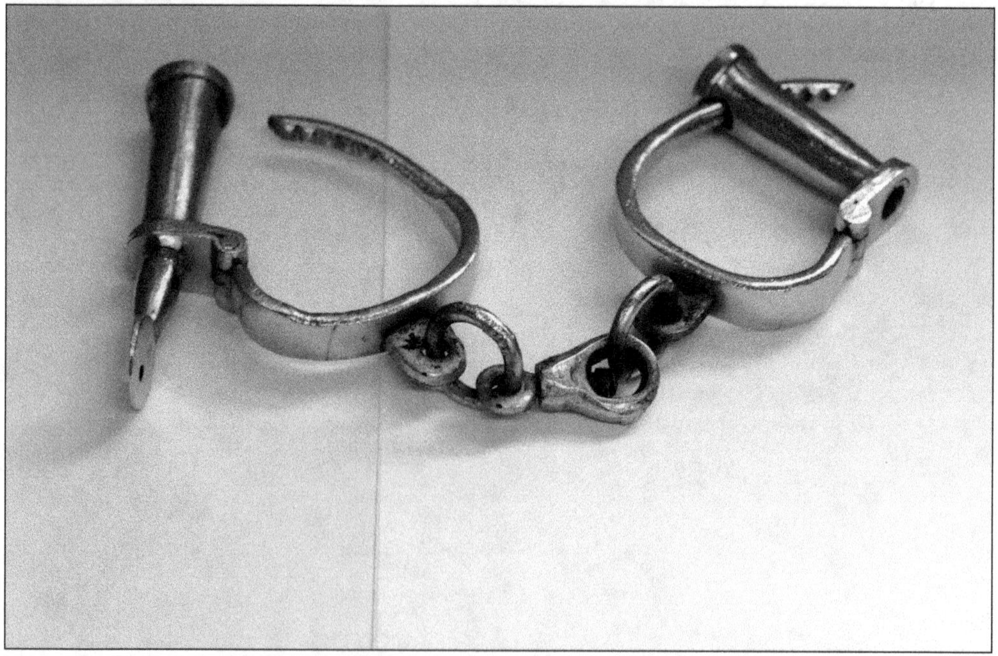

These Darby-style handcuffs would have to be unlocked, placed on the prisoners' wrists, and then relocked. This is unlike modern-day handcuffs, when the normal procedure is to subdue the subject before proceeding with cuffing. Modern, ratchet-style handcuffs have since replaced the older style of cuffs. (Courtesy of the Bikofsky collection.)

An unidentified sergeant poses for this photograph in his winter uniform around 1915. (Courtesy of the Bikofsky collection.)

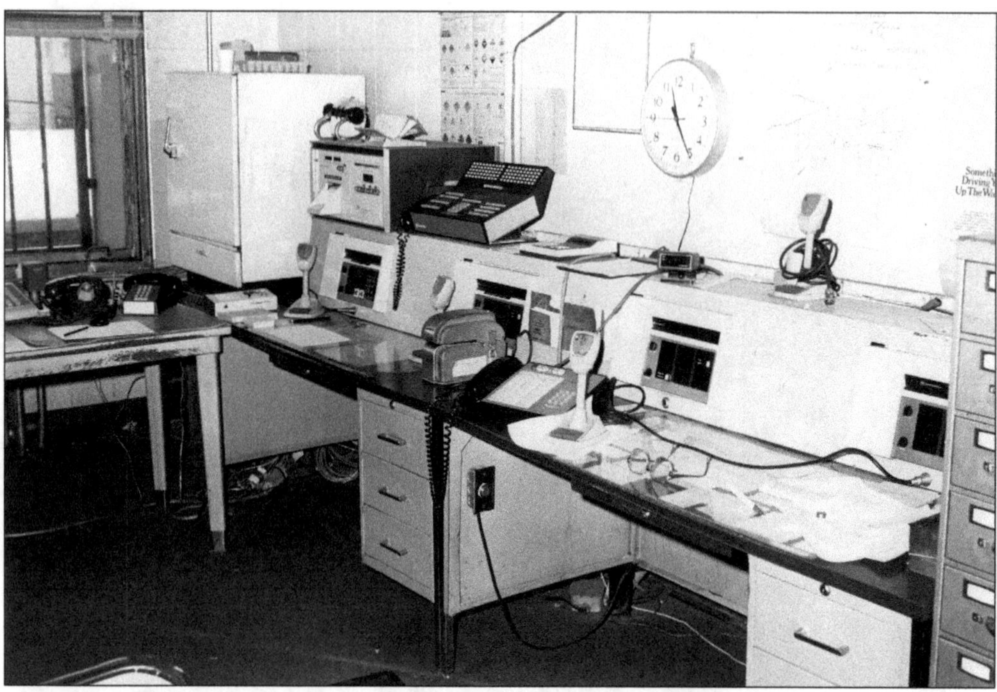

This photograph depicts the old communication center, located in police headquarters at 5 Western Avenue, which was utilized by the department prior to the opening of the Chief Leo F. Davenport Communication Center in 1981. (Courtesy of the Cambridge Police Identification Unit.)

Between the years of 1947 and 1967, those who called the Cambridge Police Department at telephone number University 4-9800, may remember the switchboard operator Catherine M. Metevier, shown here in a 1963 photograph cheerfully performing her job. (Courtesy of Kate Conway.)

This 1964 photograph shows patrolman Harry Flemming on a night shift presiding over the radio dispatching area, the nerve center of the Cambridge Police Headquarters. An emergency call to UN 4-1212 was broadcast instantly to the radio patrol cars covering all sections of the city. When street officers made their required 45-minute check-in, officer Flemming recorded it on the log sheet. (Courtesy of the Cambridge Police Identification Unit.)

Officer Francis Foster, appointed to the department in 1939, enlisted in the United States Navy in 1942, rising to the rank of lieutenant. Upon his discharge in 1947, he returned to his duties and was subsequently promoted to the rank of sergeant in 1967 and placed in charge of the department's radio equipment. The "Radio Man" is seen sitting in his office among the equipment he used to assure that the police radios were kept in proper working order at all times. (Courtesy of the Cambridge Police Identification Unit.)

Officers Edward "Butch" Hammonds, Thomas Donohue, Paul White, and Lorraine Betts pause for this photograph in 1982 while working at the new $620,000 Chief Leo F. Davenport Communication Center at the Central Square station. This state-of-the-art communication system used computers to catch criminals. It was one of the first such centers operating in any city in the state. (Courtesy of the Cambridge Police Identification Unit.)

Officer Charles Sullivan is seen in this 1940 photograph assisting pedestrians and directing traffic from the police booth in Central Square. (Courtesy of the Cambridge Historical Commission.)

Officer Charles O. Martin, who retired in 1957, is seen in Harvard Square directing traffic from the traffic booth in the early 1950s. (Courtesy of the Cambridge Historical Commission.)

In 1965, the Cambridge Police Academy was located on the second floor of the old police station at 5 Western Avenue. In addition to Cambridge officers, recruits from local police departments attended the academy, learning first aid, self-defense, criminal law, traffic law, and other police protocol. The academy class lasted for five weeks. In the early 1970s, the academy moved from this room to the basement of the Cambridge City Hospital. The room in this picture then became the identification unit for the police department. (Courtesy of the Cambridge Police Identification Unit.)

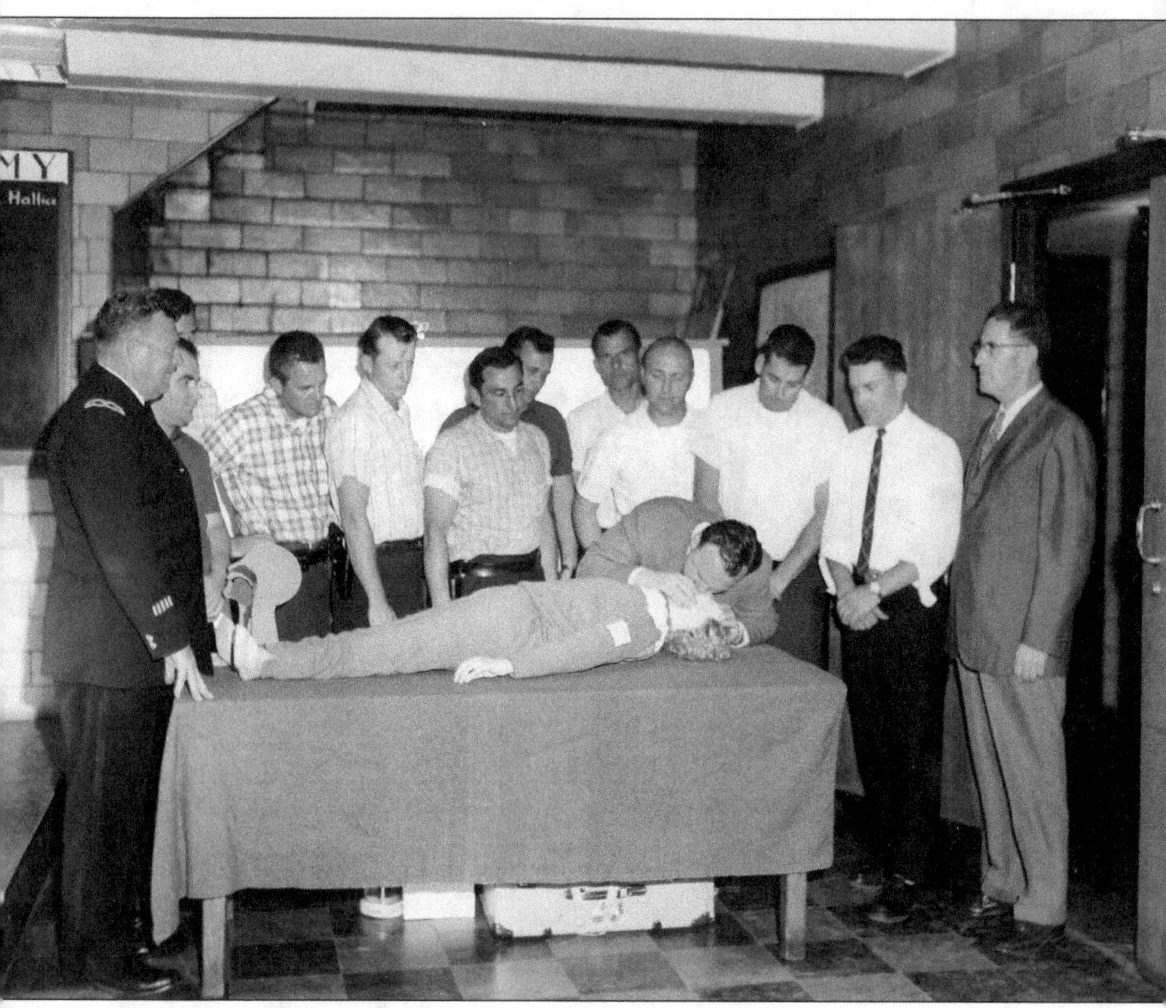

In 1962, recruits attend the training academy and are shown the proper procedure for cardiopulmonary resuscitation. From left to right are Capt. Chester Hallice, John Daly, Edward Graham, John McDonald, Leo Derveshian, Richard Parker, Harold Curll, Anthony Guida, Charles Shea, Joseph McCarthy, and Chief Daniel Brennan. (Courtesy of the Cambridge Police Identification Unit.)

Members of the Cambridge Police give a judo demonstration to the public in 1967 as part of their academy instruction. From left to right officers Calvin Kantor, Thomas Collins, Salvatore Fusco, and John McCarthy receive instruction from black-belt Edward Quniton. (Courtesy of the Cambridge Police Identification Unit.)

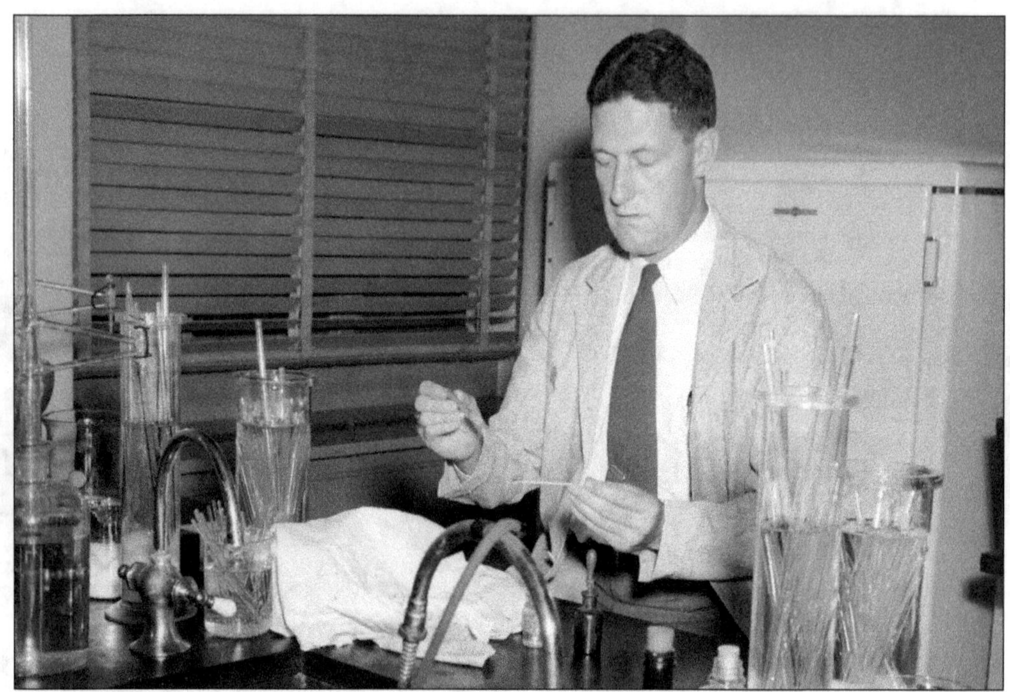
Sgt. Daniel Brennan, a member of the 25th session of the FBI's National Academy, is shown here conducting an exam of a bloodstain in the Washington, D.C., laboratory in 1944. (Courtesy of Aaron Schmidt, Boston Public Library.)

This photograph taken in 1989 depicts officer Edward Burke being trained by the Boston Police Bomb Unit. He has been a member with that unit ever since. Here he is pictured in an explosive ordnance disposal suit. This same type of suit, with some modifications, is still worn by bomb technicians at police departments across the country. (Courtesy of Edward Burke.)

Capt. James Reagan (standing) instructs (from left to right) officers George Nelson, William Maher, Joseph Grainger, John McCarthy, Paul Cloran, Fred Marckini, Lawrence Brutti, Edward O'Callaghan, unidentified, and Patrick Corcoran during firearms qualification at Camp Curtis Guild in Wakefield. (Courtesy of the Cambridge Police Identification Unit.)

Officer Woodrow (Woody) Curtis practices with his Smith and Wesson .38 revolver at Camp Curtis Guild in Wakefield. His stance here was the proper procedure for pointing and shooting at the target during the 1960s. He was appointed to the department in 1953 and retired in 1982. (Courtesy of the Cambridge Police Identification Unit.)

Officer Carl Sparre shows the proper procedure for using a barricaded point-and-shoot technique at Uncle Russ's Gas Station in North Cambridge in 1962. (Courtesy of the Cambridge Police Identification Unit.)

New officers Alvie Gosby (left) and Paul Banks (center) on the grounds of the city infirmary receive firearms instruction from Lt. Chester Hallice (right), director of the police academy in 1961. (Courtesy of Kate Conway.)

Officers receive instruction on the proper use of the submachine gun at Camp Curtis Guild in Wakefield in this early-1970s photograph. Holding the guns from left to right are officers Walter Boyle, James Lyons, Edward MacAskill, and Beni Cappello. (Courtesy of Joseph and Leona Grainger.)

In this 1938 photograph, a Cambridge police officer responds to a call for assistance at the gas station at Portland and Main Streets. (Courtesy of Joseph and Leona Grainger.)

Cambridge police officers pose at 5 Western Avenue with their new patrol wagon in this 1940s photograph. On the left is an unidentified officer, with officer Peter J. "Toby" Lyons in the center and officer Raymond Mills on the right. (Courtesy of the Cambridge Historical Commission.)

New radio patrol cars were put into service in Cambridge in 1961. Among these new vehicles was a station wagon, which could be used in an emergency as an ambulance. Patrolman Edward J. Lyons (left) and patrolman Joseph Jarvis (right) are shown checking the equipment in car 5, which patrolled the North Cambridge area. (Courtesy of Kate Conway.)

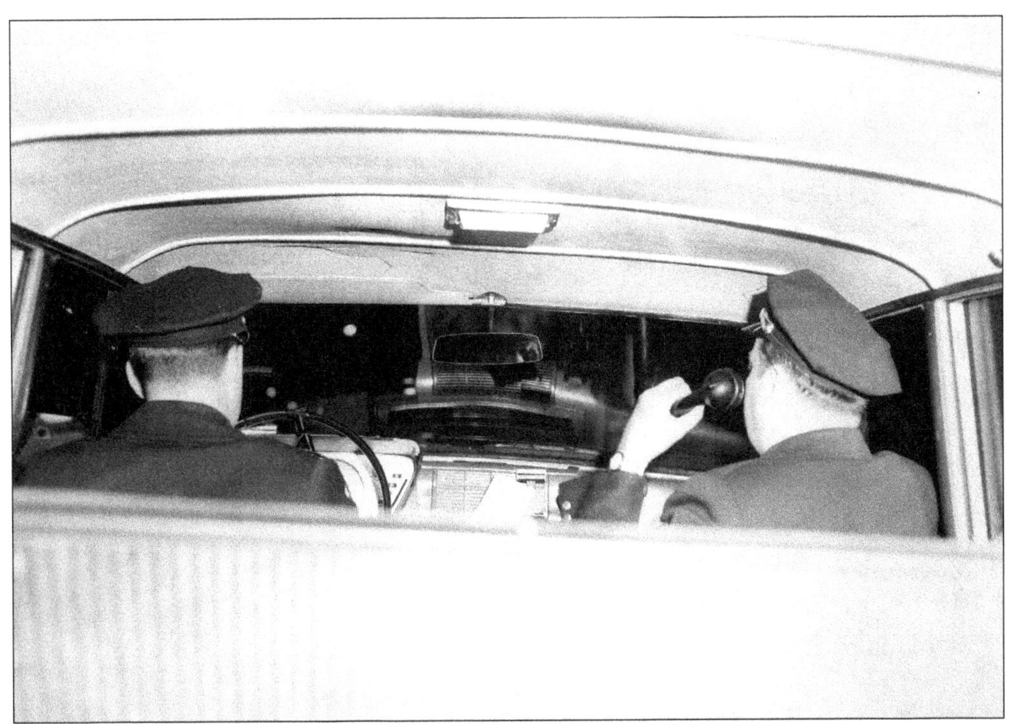

In 1963, patrolman James J. McDevitt drives the patrol car as Sgt. John P. McMahon receives a radio call from dispatchers at the 5 Western Avenue headquarters. (Courtesy of Kate Conway.)

Sgt. Thomas Egan with flashlight in hand checks the door of a garage with his partner Mauro Bombino in 1963. (Courtesy of Kate Conway.)

The cruiser in this photograph is a 2008 Ford Crown Victoria police inceptor, equipped with LED light bars on the roof. The cruiser is outfitted with a multichannel 800 megahertz, trunked radio system and includes an external public address system for making announcements. Shown here is the traditional black-and-white color scheme with a clean, modern decal set, made from highly reflective material that gives the vehicle a unique look. The cruiser is also equipped with a laptop, built to military specifications for shock resistance and temperature extremes. The laptops are connected to a secured wireless network that allows officers to access multiple information sources such as drivers' license and vehicle registration status, warrants, and the department's records management system, which allows officers to enter reports and access other databases without having to leave their vehicle. (Courtesy of the Bikofsky collection.)

Four

EARLY YEARS

This photograph is of unidentified Cambridge police officers in front of a police station house in an unknown location in the 1860s. (Courtesy of the Cambridge Historical Commission.)

Taken in 1875, this photograph depicts members of the Cambridge Police Department standing in front of station 2 located at 5 Western Avenue. From left to right are (first row) patrolman Lothrop J. Cloyes, Sgt. Andrew Sproul, Capt. Timothy Ames, and patrolmen Andrew J. Smith and Leonard Shackford; (second row) unidentified, patrolmen Alonzo Harriman, Benjamin Kennard, Micha Cook, Hugh McNamee, James Munroe, and Frederick B. Pullen; (third row) patrolmen William Evans, William Fitzpatrick, and Patrick Doyle. (Courtesy of the Cambridge Historical Commission.)

Members of the Cambridge Police Department's District 1 in Harvard Square pose outside their newly constructed police station in 1877. The station was located at 108 Mount Auburn Street in Brattle Square. From left to right are (first row) officers Hamman, Sproul, Mullet, and Copeland, Chief Ames, and officers Cook, Cloyes, and Shackford; (second row) officers Fitzpatrick, Miller, MacNamee, Pullen, Smith, Cook, Marshal, and Morse; (third row) officers Brown, Kennard, Evans, Cleveland, Penny, Doyle, Morse, and Callahan. (Courtesy of the Cambridge Historical Commission.)

Members of the Cambridge Police Department pose for this official photograph outside their station house in 1880. (Courtesy of the Cambridge Historical Commission.)

This photograph of a horse-drawn police wagon was taken in 1883 at station 3 located at 34 Fourth Street, currently known as Schirappa Street. (Courtesy of the Cambridge Historical Commission.)

Two unknown Cambridge police officers are on foot patrol in front of city hall in Central Square around 1915. (Courtesy of the Cambridge Historical Commission.)

In this pre-1896 photograph, a lone officer stands guard outside police station 4, which was previously located at 34 Fourth Street in East Cambridge. Members of the Cambridge Fire Department stop to pose for this picture as they make their way down the street, accompanying the fire wagon. Police station 4 closed its doors in 1942 after all the police stations were centralized into one building. (Courtesy of the Cambridge Historical Commission.)

Members of the Cambridge Police Department are seen here in a picture taken around 1915. Standing in the center of the back row is Jeremiah McCarthy who, after being appointed on April 7, 1886, served the department for 39 years. (Courtesy of the Cambridge Historical Commission.)

This photograph was taken on the Lawrence Common on March 19, 1919. It depicts members of the Cambridge Police Department who worked with other surrounding departments to assist the Lawrence Police during the Lawrence Textile Strike of 1919. This strike was one of the most significant labor protests of the early 1900s and resulted from the workers' desire to secure a 48-hour workweek without a reduction in pay. The strike took place from February 3 until May 20, when the issue was finally resolved in the union's favor. Standing on the far left at the end is officer Timothy J. Toomey. The other officers cannot be identified. (Photograph by George H. Leck, courtesy of Dr. Timothy Toomey.)

In this undated photograph of Cambridge police officers from the 1920s, standing at the far right is officer Timothy J. Toomey. Officer Toomey was appointed in 1917, promoted to sergeant in 1948, and retired in 1955. During his 38-year career, he received 11 commendations from various chiefs. (Courtesy of Dr. Timothy Toomey.)

This *c.* 1922 picture depicts an officer in Harvard Square directing traffic. Prior to the installation of the traffic signal system throughout the city, officers were assigned to key locations to help expedite the movement of traffic. (Courtesy of Cambridge Historical Society, George G. Wright Collection.)

Officers pose for this late-1920s photograph in full uniform in front of the old station 2 on Western Avenue. (Courtesy of the Cambridge Historical Commission.)

Seen in this photograph taken on June 13, 1936, are, from left to right, (first row) officers McMahon, Chester Hallice, Thomas Brown, Chief Daniel Lahey, "Sugar" Gannon, and Gerald McCarthy; (second row) Joseph Gould, Francis Barry, Joseph Bateman, Daniel Coleman, and Matthew Higgins. (Courtesy of the Cambridge Police Identification Unit.)

This photograph was taken on July 3, 1925, during the Cambridge Police Platoon civic parade. At the time, officers were mandated to participate in these types of events. Some of the obstacles that officers faced in 1925 were the nonexistence of radios, teletypes, vehicles, and even training. Their pay was $29 per week. Chief John J. McBride led the parade pictured here, on the left. Sgt. Robert F. Douglas stands next to him on the right. Also seen are patrolman Thomas

O'Loughlin (7th from left); patrolman John R. King (9th from left), who later became the chief of police; patrolman Charles Linehan (11th from left); patrolman Richard Linehan (12th from left); reserveman Edward P. Glennon (5th from right); patrolman Joseph P. Breen (4th from right), and patrolman Dennis W. O'Brien (3rd from right). At the end on the right is officer Timothy Toomey. (Courtesy of Sgt. Richard Linehan.)

This photograph was taken across the street from the old police station at 5 Western Avenue in the late 1940s. From left to right are officer John Silva, registry inspector Daniel Doyle, and officer Joseph Hayes. The Olympia Theater in the background, designed by architect Charles Greco, was in operation from 1910 to 1954. Today it is the site of Veteran's Memorial Park, dedicated in 1999. (Courtesy of the Cambridge Historical Commission.)

This 1947 recruit class became known as the "Class of Brass" for its advancement in the department. From left to right are (first row) Chief John King, officer William Killion, officer Joseph Lynch, Lt. James O'Leary, Lt. John Holian, Sgt. John Horgan, and Sgt. Daniel Brennan; (second row) officer William Story, Capt. Joseph Cusack, Capt. Joseph Grainger, Capt. Lawrence Brutti, and Capt. James Sugrue; (third row) officer Peter Strozi, Chief Leo Davenport, Sgt. Duncan McNeil, Sgt. John McCarthy, and officer Robert Mahoney. (Courtesy of the Cambridge Police Identification Unit.)

From left to right, officers John Mearn, Edward Loder, James Hallice, Ernie Lowe, Donald Carney, William Lyons, and Sgt. John Horgan seem pretty relaxed as they pose for this late-1960s photograph. (Photograph by Deputy Chief Paul Upton, courtesy of Mary Horgan.)

Taken in March 1960, this academy class is made up of Cambridge and Wakefield recruits. The five Cambridge recruits are seated to the right of the photograph. In the center is Richard Umanzio. Directly behind him is Patrick Keating. Second from the right is Daniel Tulley. Directly behind him is William Burke. On the far right is Thomas Gliesman. At the time the officers attended five weeks of intensive training, including law, weapons, and first-aid. (Courtesy of the Cambridge Police Identification Unit.)

In July 1975, 28 officers were promoted to the rank of sergeant, making them the largest group of officers to be promoted to the rank of sergeant at one time. From left to right are (first row) Mayor Walter Sullivan, police chief Francis Pisani, and city manager James Leo Sullivan; (second row) George Powers, Irwin Nolan, William Cummings, Timothy Lane, Harold Murphy, Walter Boyle, and Donald Carney; (third row) John Walsh, Ronald Eillis, Joseph Amoroso, Ronald Briand, Calvin Kantor Sr., Mitchell Babajtis, and Richard Ring; (fourth row) Dennis McCarthy, Dominic Scalese, Timothy Toomey, Orlando Yemma, Oresto Tirimacio, and Richard Cahill; (fifth row) Richard Scott, Allen Hayes, James Hallice, and Christopher Patsio; (sixth row) Fidele Centrella, Thomas Benson, Herbert Halliday Jr., and James McDevitt. (Photograph by Edward Pacheco, courtesy of Calvin Kantor Sr.)

Officer Albert G. Eckardt, a decorated World War II army veteran, was appointed to the department in 1941. On November 11, 1951, just a few short months after this roll call roster assigning him to Route 8 was distributed, officer Eckardt was tragically killed in an automobile collision between the police ambulance he was riding in and two private cars. He was the third police officer killed in the line of duty. The department has named the police commendation medal in his honor. (Courtesy of Sgt. Peter Marfione.)

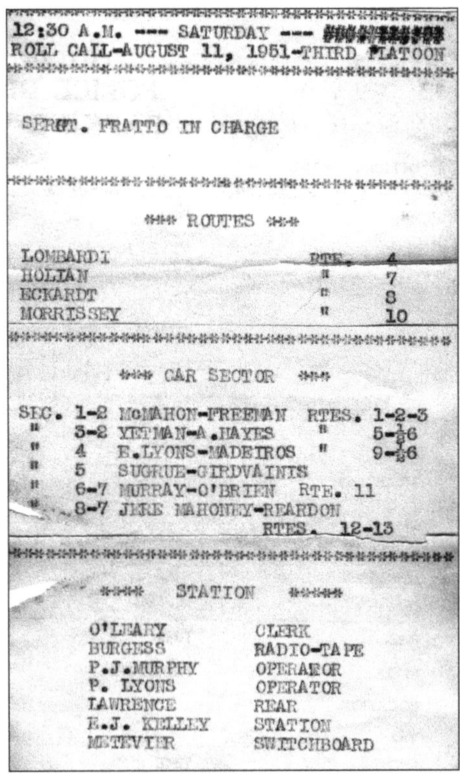

12:30 A.M. --- SATURDAY ---
ROLL CALL-AUGUST 11, 1951-THIRD PLATOON

SERGT. FRATTO IN CHARGE

*** ROUTES ***

LOMBARDI	RTE.	4
HOLIAN	"	7
ECKARDT	"	8
MORRISSEY	"	10

*** CAR SECTOR ***

SEC.	1-2	McMAHON-FREEMAN	RTES.	1-2-3
"	3-2	YETMAN-A.HAYES	"	5-½6
"	4	E.LYONS-MADEIROS	"	9-½6
"	5	SUGRUE-GIRDVAINIS		
"	6-7	MURRAY-O'BRIEN	RTE.	11
"	8-7	JERE MAHONEY-REARDON	RTES.	12-13

**** STATION ****

O'LEARY	CLERK
BURGESS	RADIO-TAPE
P.J.MURPHY	OPERATOR
P. LYONS	OPERATOR
LAWRENCE	REAR
E.J. KELLEY	STATION
METEVIER	SWITCHBOARD

In the 1960s, the Cambridge Police created missing persons posters using a sheet of tin metal. This particular posting describes a 33-year-old female who went missing and possibly ran off to Louisiana or Texas. The husband of the missing woman feared that she might have been taken there against her will. (Courtesy of officer Thomas Grainger.)

General Order No. 14, Series of 1963
Effective 12:01 A. M. - Monday 7/1/63

PAID POLICE DETAILS

WEEKDAYS

	Minimum Three Hours	*Each Hour or portion thereof in excess of Three Hours*
Patrolman	$12.00	$3.50
Sergeant	$14.00	$4.00
Lieutenant	$16.00	$4.50
Captain	$18.00	$5.00

SUNDAYS - LEGAL HOLIDAYS AFTER MIDNIGHT

	Minimum Three Hours	*Each Hour or portion thereof in excess of Three Hours*
Patrolman	$14.00	$4.00
Sergeant	$16.00	$4.50
Lieutenant	$18.00	$5.00
Captain	$20.00	$5.50

Per Order
Daniel J. Brennan
Chief of Police

This general order shows the pay scale for the various ranks when performing a paid detail in 1963. Over the past 45 years, the rates have increased substantially: patrolman from $12 per hour to $38, sergeant from $14 to $43, lieutenant from $16 to $45, and captain from $18 to $47. (Courtesy of Mary Horgan.)

This identification badge belonged to Richard J. Linehan. It was the type of identification carried prior to 1975 by Cambridge police officers, who were required to carry it at all times. On July 23, 1966, officer Linehan responded to a bank alarm to find an armed robbery in progress. Officer Linehan ordered one of the suspects, who was holding the manager at gunpoint, to drop his weapon. The suspect turned on the officer, who shot him in the shoulder. Officer Linehan was subsequently commended for his bravery in the apprehension of the suspect. (Courtesy of Sgt. Richard Linehan.)

The Prospect Union Building was located at 750 Massachusetts Avenue at the corner of Pleasant Street. It was built on land donated by Edmund T. Dana in 1850 and used as Cambridge City Hall beginning in 1854. The first police station was located in the basement of this building until 1873, when a new police station was built at 5 Western Avenue. In 1899, city hall moved to its current location at 795 Massachusetts Avenue. The Prospect building was demolished in 1922. (Courtesy of the Cambridge Historical Commission.)

Police station 4, located at 2101–2103 Massachusetts Avenue, was originally built in 1868 to serve as a firehouse, wardroom, meeting hall, and neighborhood police station. It also served as a branch library until the early 1920s. Cambridge's neighborhood police stations were closed in 1942. This building was soon leased to a veterans' post, and it continued in this capacity into the mid-1990s. (Courtesy of the Cambridge Historical Commission.)

Old station 2, located at the corner of Western Avenue and Green Street, was built in 1873 at a cost of $85,000. It was destroyed by fire in 1932 and replaced by a new state-of-the-art police headquarters in 1933 that remained in use through 2008. (Courtesy of the Cambridge Historical Commission.)

This photograph of station 1, located at the south side of 108 Mount Auburn Street, was taken in 1880. This large brick building was erected in 1876 at a cost of about $75,000. The building was used as a police court, police station, engine house, ward meetinghouse, several city offices, art school, and day school. It was removed from service in 1935 upon the completion of the new headquarters at 5 Western Avenue and demolished soon thereafter. (Courtesy of the Cambridge Historical Society.)

Longtime partners John J. Grainger (left) and William Arnold Doyle (right) are seen here in this 1952 photograph outside their police vehicle in East Cambridge. Both officers received numerous commendations throughout their careers. Officer Doyle received one such commendation in 1946 when a North Cambridge man shot and killed his wife. After an APB (all points bulletin) was broadcast, officer Doyle observed the suspect and gave chase, apprehending him at Massachusetts Avenue and Dana Street still in possession of the murder weapon, a Walther automatic pistol. (Courtesy of Joseph and Leona Grainger.)

This 1962 photograph depicts the unusual art deco–style police station at 5 Western Avenue that was built in 1933 at a cost of approximately $286,926. It then served as the main police headquarters when the substations in North and East Cambridge were finally closed. It was originally built as a municipal building for city offices, housing a VFW American Legion and the election commission as well as the police department. (Courtesy of the Cambridge Police Department.)

On December 8, 2008, the Cambridge Police Department moved from its Central Square location, a home that had served it well for 135 years. The new location of the department is this ultramodern, 100,000-square-foot, $60 million, state-of-the-art building located at 125 Sixth Street in East Cambridge. The Robert W. Healy Public Safety Facility will also be utilized to house the city's emergency communication center. (Courtesy of Robert Marshall.)

Five

After Hours

Officers of the Cambridge Police Department salute the casket of retired police captain Michael J. Brennan as his remains are carried into St. John's Catholic Church in North Cambridge. Captain Brennan was appointed to the department on April 14, 1884, and served for 52 years before retiring on October 8, 1936, at the age of 79. In March 1938, as Captain Brennan walked down the street, he brushed against Henry A. Sterling, 21, of Somerville, accidentally knocking off his hat. Sterling assaulted the captain, and he was hospitalized as a result of the attack. Captain Brennan died three weeks later due to the injuries he sustained, with his five sons and two daughters at his bedside. (Courtesy of Charles Sullivan.)

Cambridge police officers mourn the death of police chief Daniel Brennan, a 36-year veteran, who died suddenly on September 9, 1967. Fifteen hundred mourners lined St. Peter's Church on Concord Avenue to pay their final respects to the fallen leader of the department. (Courtesy of Joseph and Leona Grainger.)

Chief John J. Grainger is seen here in this 1968 photograph with his two sons, Lt. Joseph Grainger (center) and Sgt. John Grainger Jr. (right). The Graingers' dedicated service to the citizens of Cambridge dates backs to 1930. Lieutenant Grainger was later promoted to captain and served as the acting police chief before his retirement in 1991. Sergeant Grainger's son Thomas Grainger was the police department's officer of the year in 2004. (Courtesy of Joseph and Leona Grainger.)

In 1967, members of the traffic unit provide a funeral escort riding Vespa police model motor scooters. The Vespa scooter had the ability to cruise at speeds from 2 miles per hour to 65 miles per hour. In addition, the operation of this scooter cost 2.5¢ per mile versus 16¢ per mile for a motorcycle, as well as holding a mileage record of over 100 miles to the gallon. The Vespa combined the advantages of a walking officer and cost pennies a day to operate, making it very popular among police departments throughout the United States in the late 1960s. (Courtesy of the Cambridge Police Identification Unit.)

The Cambridge Police Honor Guard marches in front of police headquarters during the funeral procession of patrolman Lawrence Hector, escorting him to his final resting place in the early 1980s. (Courtesy of the Cambridge Police Identification Unit.)

Officers Timothy O'Brien (left), William Arthur (center), and John Albert (right) pose for this photograph outside St. John's Church following a funeral service in 1998. Ten years later, all three officers remain members of the traffic unit, currently known as the selective enforcement unit. Officer Albert was promoted to sergeant in 2000, and to lieutenant in 2003 and placed in charge of the selective enforcement unit. Officer William Arthur's grandfather Samuel Arthur served the department for 37 years from 1923 to 1960. (Photograph by Edward Fowler.)

The officer standing on the left is Richard J. Linehan, and on the right is Sgt. John Horgan, who represented the Cambridge Police Department in raising money for the memorial fund of Massachusetts State Police trooper Edward A. Mahoney. The trooper was killed during a motor vehicle stop on November 21, 1976, when his patrol car was struck from behind. Years before his death, he received a Lifesaving Award for rescuing a motorist trapped in a burning vehicle. (Courtesy of Mary Horgan.)

Cambridge police officers march down Memorial Drive in this 1916 photograph. (Courtesy of the Bikofsky collection.)

Police march to church and a communion breakfast in May 1962, a tradition that began in 1938. (Courtesy of Joseph and Leona Grainger.)

On January 19, 1955, officer George Donovan of the Cambridge Police (front, left) clears the way for a National Guard tank from Fort Devens, sent by Massachusetts governor Christian Herter to quell a prisoner uprising at the Massachusetts State Prison in Charlestown. Prisoners Walter Harold Balben, a gunman serving 35 to 49 years; Theodore (Teddy) Green, a major suspect in the famous Brinks Robbery serving 45 to 52 years; Joseph "Red" Flaherty, a rapist serving 35 to 47 years; and Fritz Swenson, a cop killer serving a life sentence, captured five prison guards and held them hostage in the section of the prison known as Cherry Hill. Teddy Green's teenaged daughter, Toby, eventually persuaded her father to surrender, which ended the 85-hour standoff. Green was sent to Alcatraz after the riot and later bragged of robbing 20 banks and making 40 prison break attempts. (Courtesy of officer George Donovan III.)

Members of the Cambridge Police Department march in the Memorial Day parade in May 1976. (Courtesy of Joseph and Leona Grainger.)

The Cambridge Police Honor Guard marches down Massachusetts Avenue during National Police Week in May 1992. This parade traveled from Memorial Drive to city hall and into Harvard Square. The honor guard has always been a volunteer unit, participating in funerals for fallen officers throughout New England and beyond. The honor guard has even traveled internationally to represent the department in other countries. (Courtesy of the Cambridge Police Identification Unit.)

Officer Samuel Arthur, a member of the traffic squad, is seen in this late-1920s photograph with children in Putnam Square. Officer Arthur was appointed to the department on September 23, 1923, and retired on September 20, 1960, after 37 years of dedicated service. (Courtesy of the Cambridge Historical Commission.)

Sgt. Daniel Brennan presents an award to 13-year-old safety patrol director John Gannon of St. Paul's School for protecting another child from harm in 1947. (Courtesy of Aaron Schmidt, Boston Public Library.)

Members of the Cambridge Police Department are representing the Irish American Police Officers Association at the first annual Ahern Family Charitable Foundation dinner in 2002. The foundation has raised over $250,000 to benefit homeless veterans. From left to right are detective Sarah Drewicz, officers Kathy Sullivan, Edward Burke, Sgt. Edward O'Callaghan, and officer Sean Tierney, who in 2007 was named Cambridge Police Officer of the Year. (Courtesy of Edward Burke.)

In 1942, the city council passed an ordinance accepting the state law that required registrations of bicycles, and the traffic bureau issued 4,393 registrations that year. In this photograph, Sgt. John Grainger shows a young lady how to properly display her bicycle license plate. (Courtesy of Joseph and Leona Grainger.)

This 1963 photograph depicts Sgt. James O'Leary with an unidentified woman promoting the Cambridge Vaccination Program SABIN, an oral polio vaccine, sponsored by the Cambridge Health Department. (Photograph by Edward F. Carry, courtesy of Kate Conway.)

This Jeep Wrangler was donated by the Rigazio Brothers, a former automotive dealer in the city of Cambridge. Driven by officer Paul Xavier, "Friendly Sam," as the jeep was called, drove around to meet with the residents of Cambridge, primarily children, and taught them about safety. This early form of community policing took place throughout the mid-1970s. (Courtesy of Edward Burke.)

Susan Cunningham, assistant vice president of the East Cambridge Savings Bank, lifts Erin McCabe of Medford to hug their friend the robot, the newest recruit of the Cambridge Police Department purchased with a major grant from the bank. (Courtesy of the Cambridge Police Identification Unit.)

On March 6, 1934, Cambridge police officers and local city officials attended a farewell party for the closing of the Brattle Square police station, which was located at 108 Mount Auburn Street. The building was constructed in 1876. (Courtesy of the Cambridge Historical Commission.)

This photograph was taken on February 24, 1943, at Memorial Hall, Harvard University, during one of the first auxiliary police banquets. The Cambridge Auxiliary Police was formed on December 10, 1941, three days after the bombing of Pearl Harbor. As a show of appreciation for

these volunteer officers, the mayor of the city of Cambridge continues to hold an annual banquet for them and their families each year. (Courtesy of the Cambridge Historical Commission.)

The 83rd annual Cambridge Police Ball was held at the Hotel Continental in 1955. Seen from left to right are Captain and Mrs. Edward F. Tierney, Chief and Mrs. Patrick F. Ready, and Lieutenant and Mrs. Chester F. Hallice. (Courtesy of Aaron Schmidt, Boston Public Library.)

A retirement dinner was held at the Fresh Pond Grill on November 21, 1957, for Chief Patrick F. Ready, who was appointed to the department as a patrolman in 1916 and promoted to sergeant in 1928, lieutenant in 1939, captain in 1947, and chief on October 10, 1951. From left to right are (first row) Dr. John Ready (his son), Chief Patrick F. Ready, Michael Neville (former mayor and toastmaster), and Rev. Francis P. Ready (his son); (second row) Congressman Thomas P. O'Neil, Robert B. Watson (dean of Harvard), Capt. Richard J. Linehan, and John B. Atkinson (former city manager). During Chief Ready's 41-year police career, he was commended on eight separate occasions. (Photograph by Ernest McClean, courtesy of Aaron Schmidt, Boston Public Library.)

Chief Daniel Brennan (center) poses with the board members of the Cambridge Police Mutual Aid Association at its annual ball in 1959. From left to right are detective Paul Cloran (secretary), Sgt. Joseph Cusack (vice president), Chief Brennan, officer Francis McCusker (president), and Lt. Joseph Bateman (treasurer). (Courtesy of Aaron Schmidt, Boston Public Library.)

Members of the Cambridge Police Department are at the police banquet in 1959. On the right, seated is patrolman Lawrence W. Gorman, who was killed in the performance of his duty on September 3, 1960. (Photograph by Dan Murphy, courtesy of Carl Sparre.)

In this 1962 photograph, Charles H. Cremens (left), director of health and safety in the Cambridge schools, presents Mayor Edward A. Crane with a special award given to the City of Cambridge for outstanding performance in school safety education by the National Safety Council, while Michael E. Whelan of the Massachusetts Safety Council and Sgt. John McCarthy, school traffic education officer of the police department, look on. (Photograph by the Cambridge Police Identification Unit.)

Members of the Cambridge Police Department and Lowell Police Department pose for this photograph at a local baseball game on August 13, 1895. The Cambridge Police members on the team are seated while the Lowell Police members (with "LP" clearly marked on their shirts) are standing behind them. (Courtesy of the Cambridge Historical Commission.)

In 1950, the Cambridge Police softball team finished second in the Suburban League with 17 wins and 5 loses. Here the team prepares to play a game at St. Peter's Field on Sherman Street. From left to right are (first row) Fred Clancy, Dominic Scalese, bat boy John Parker, Sidney Hynes, and Frank Pilieri; (second row) bat boy Robert Stow, Daniel Walsh, Alfred Lange, Michael Lombardi, team captain Joseph Ford, John Paine, Ben Silva, and umpire Joseph Mills. (Courtesy of Alfred Lange.)

In 1991, the sponsor of the Cambridge Police softball team, John Courtney (standing left), with Mayor Francis H. Duehay (to the right of Courtney), poses with members of the team, from left to right, (first row) Edward O'Callaghan, Peter Marfione, William Frammartino Sr., ball boy Richard Bongiorno Jr. with dad Richard Bongiorno Sr., Lester Sullivan, and John Murphy; (second row) Robert Ames, Henry Korecki, Charles Mottola, Michael Giacoppo, Steven Williams, and Stephen Hall. (Courtesy of Deputy Steven Williams.)

In 1981, the Cambridge Police Stirs won the police suburban state championship. From left to right are (first row) James Hite, Patrick Nagle, and Leonard DiPietro; (second row) Timothy McCusker, Henry Korecki, Lloyd Lewis, Lawrence Stead, David Degou, James Hallice, and Edward O'Callaghan. (Courtesy of James Hallice.)

In this photograph taken in 1939, members of the United States Fat Man's Club celebrate their annual banquet. The club dates back to the late 19th century. Cambridge police officer John "Harry" Bagan (third from the left) was president of the United States Fat Man's Club for many years. Standing at the far right is police officer John Cahalane, who retired in 1942 after a long and distinguished career with the Cambridge Police Department. (Courtesy of Shawn Dolan-Tavares.)

Six

Notable Events

In this 1925 photograph, officers of the Cambridge Police Department conduct a raid of an unlicensed liquor establishment. During the Prohibition era, many raids such as this one were often conducted. From left to right are Patrick "Buster" Ready, Capt. Patrick Lahey, detective Thomas "Rocks" Leary, officer Timothy Callaghan, and an unidentified patrolman. (Courtesy of the Cambridge Historical Commission.)

The Cambridge Police Department and the Secret Service provide dignitary protection for president-elect John F. Kennedy in January 1961 as he arrives at Harvard University for a meeting of the board of overseers. (Courtesy of Joseph and Leona Grainger.)

A smiling Pres. John F. Kennedy is protected by a large security detail on his visit to Cambridge and Harvard University in 1962. From left to right in the first row are detectives Joseph Cellucci, John Grainger, Sgt. Joseph Hayes, and detective Dominic Scalese. (Courtesy of Joseph and Leona Grainger.)

Cambridge police officers Thomas Reid (left) and Sgt. Patrick Corcoran escort Rev. Martin Luther King during his visit to Cambridge in April 1967. Reverend King was to speak at Harvard University. (Courtesy of the Cambridge Police Identification Unit.)

Members of the Cambridge Police Tactical Patrol Force are seen here in this 2004 photograph on the banks of the Charles River during the Democratic National Convention. The unit, created during the social unrest of the 1960s, is still highly trained and motivated today. Standing on the far left is the tactical patrol force commander Lt. Paul Ames. (Courtesy of Sgt. George Sabby.)

In 1970, Sgt. Henry Gallagher (left) of the Cambridge Police Department talks with protesters in Harvard Square as members of the tactical patrol force stand by with riot guns. (Photograph by Jack Fallon, courtesy of Aaron Schmidt, Boston Public Library.)

In this May 1970 photograph, a sea of protesters blocks Boylston Street (now JFK Street) in a tense standoff between themselves and members of the tactical patrol force. Many surrounding cities and towns, including the state police, assisted Cambridge in quelling the riot. (Courtesy of Sgt. John Boyle.)

Sgt. Henry Gallagher of the tactical patrol force appears to be alone among protesters, who are keeping their distance, as he attempts to extinguish a barrel fire set by antiwar protesters in Harvard Square in 1970. (Courtesy of Sgt. John Boyle.)

In this 1970 photograph, protesters in Harvard Square show their displeasure about the United States' growing involvement in the war in Vietnam. Thousands marched on Harvard Square, set fires, and destroyed property. Many police and civilian protesters were seriously injured during the riot that lasted nearly a week. (Courtesy of Sgt. John Boyle.)

Members of the Cambridge Police Tactical Patrol Force march down Massachusetts Avenue in formation with their riot sticks in the ready position. (Courtesy of the Cambridge Police Identification Unit.)

Members of the Cambridge Police Department's tactical patrol force try to persuade protesters of the Vietnam War to come down from atop the kiosk in Harvard Square in 1970. (Photograph by Paul Hirshon, courtesy of the Cambridge Historical Commission.)

Members of the tactical patrol force subdue a war protester in Harvard Square during the 1970 riot. Chief James Reagan awarded all members of the tactical patrol force two days off with pay and wrote that the officers' actions were "a highly commendable display of professional discipline and courage in the face of danger." (Courtesy of Sgt. John Boyle.)

Seen are the remnants of a fire-bombed Cambridge police cruiser destroyed by antiwar protesters in Harvard Square in 1970. (Courtesy of the Cambridge Police Department.)

Students protesting the United States' involvement in Vietnam in 1970 show their displeasure as they block the street in Harvard Square. (Courtesy of the Cambridge Historical Commission.)

Sgt. Anthony Paolillo is seen assisting a state police sergeant in arresting one of the students demonstrating for the abolition of the Reserve Officers' Training Corps (ROTC). Other protesters were evicted from Harvard's University Hall by force following a predawn raid by riot-equipped police in April 1969. (Courtesy of Chief Anthony Paolillo.)

On October 23, 1958, four men robbed the Middlesex County Bank in Cambridge of $107,000, making it the largest bank robbery in New England at that time. A cashier and teller were assaulted, and other bank employees were restrained. The stolen Buick in this photograph was used as their getaway car and later found abandoned on Fifth Street in East Cambridge. The two suspects initially planned the robbery while employed as a janitor and window washer at the bank. When one of these suspects was arrested for questioning regarding a separate incident, he confessed to this robbery, stating that they had thrown their guns into the river while they fled the scene. Approximately one half of the money was recovered, and the four suspects were indicted on armed robbery charges. (Courtesy of the Cambridge Police Identification Unit.)

Taken in the late 1970s, the officer in this picture, Alvie Gosby, stands patiently waiting for the patrol wagon to arrive. The suspect has been placed on the ground in this prone position after an attempted breaking and entering of a commercial establishment. (Courtesy of the Cambridge Police Identification Unit.)

Cambridge police officers are seen during an internal department hearing before Chief Timothy F. Leahy on September 2, 1943. Gasoline rationing coupons worth $40,000 were stolen from the Cambridge Rationing Office, located in the basement of the city hall. The hearing was to address whether these officers properly investigated this crime. The court subsequently dismissed all charges against the officers. From left to right are Lt. William O'Dell and attorney Chester A. Higley, attorney Francis J. Roche and his client Capt. Joseph E. Kelley, and attorney William Cunningham, defense attorney for Sgt. Mark Cunningham (not seen in the photograph). (Courtesy of Aaron Schmidt, Boston Public Library.)

Capt. Patrick Ready of the detective bureau counts the $3,700 cash recovered from a holdup of a cleaning company at 1016 Massachusetts Avenue in 1949 in which Harry P. Shea was murdered. A janitor employee was later arrested and charged with Shea's murder. (Courtesy of Aaron Schmidt, Boston Public Library.)

Shown from left to right in this 1959 photograph are detectives Charles Brady and Paul Cloran, along with Capt. John Grainger holding $20,000 in bonds recovered through an intensive investigation, earning them, and detective Edward Colleran (not seen in the photograph), a commendation that included two days off with pay. (Courtesy of Joseph and Leona Grainger.)

Officers of the Cambridge Police Department protect a crime scene at 2024 Massachusetts Avenue after a gangland style execution took place on April 10, 1972. The driver and passenger of the vehicle were killed while two others sitting in the back seat managed to survive. It was later determined that the gunshots came from a high-powered rifle across the street. The officer standing in the center of the picture is Edward Lyons, and the officer on the right side of the picture is Frederick D. D. O'Connor. (Courtesy of the Cambridge Police Identification Unit.)

This photograph was taken following a raid of a private social club on Columbia Street sometime in the early 1980s. During the investigation, detectives confiscated money, drugs, and liquor. Detective Sgt. James Roscoe stands on the left, counting money. Detective Thomas Collins is bent over to his left, and detective John Carbone, with the beard, investigates the contents of a plastic bag. They are assisted by uniformed officer Joseph Lencki, standing in the background. (Courtesy of the Cambridge Police Identification Unit.)

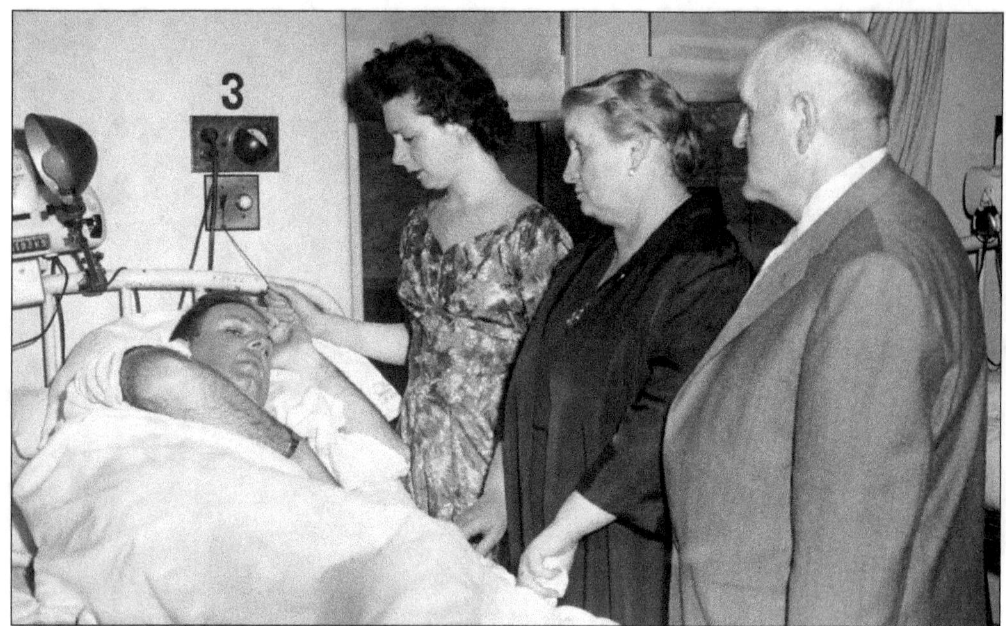

Sgt. Alfred Lange lies in his hospital bed at the Mount Auburn Hospital, with his wife Theresa, mother Flora, and father Odelius Lange by his side. Here he is recovering from a bullet wound inflicted by a robber while attempting to hold-up the A&P supermarket on Alewife Brook Parkway in 1957. Sergeant Lange made a full recovery and subsequently rose to the rank of captain within the department. (Courtesy of Aaron Schmidt, Boston Public Library.)

In this 1938 photograph, Chief Timothy Leahy announces the promotion of three sergeants to the rank of lieutenant and three patrolmen to the rank of sergeant. At that time, the yearly pay rate for a sergeant was $2,500 and that of a lieutenant was $2,750. From left to right are Lt. Thomas J. Stokes, Lt. James M. Landrigan, Lt. Wellington Bateman, Sgt. John Finnegan, Sgt. Daniel Brennan, Chief Leahy, and Sgt. Raymond L. Patten. (Courtesy of Aaron Schmidt, Boston Public Library.)

David J. Degou was born in Cambridge in 1949. He attended Northeastern University in Boston, graduating in 1974 and received his master's degree from Boston State College in 1978. He was appointed to the Cambridge Police Department on September 29, 1975. The following is the sequence of his promotions during his career with the department: sergeant in 1983, lieutenant in 1988, deputy in 1992, captain in 1994, and superintendent in 1996. (Courtesy of the Cambridge Police Identification Unit.)

In Memoriam

Fallen Officers:
Officer William Loughrey, 1860, Medal of Valor
Officer Thomas J. Riley, 1920, Lifesaving Medal
Officer Albert G. Eckardt, 1951, Police Commendation Medal
Officer Lawrence Gorman, 1960, Medal of Honor

The family of officer William J. Carroll, who died suddenly in 1975, remains devoted to the members of the Cambridge Police Department. The department honors his name each year with the presentation of the Carroll Award during National Police Week.

The family of Allen T. McPherson, who lost his life in 1930 while bravely coming to the aid of Cambridge police officer William Anderson, also remains devoted to the department. The Citizen Service Award was recently renamed the Allen T. McPherson Citizen Service Award, in his honor.

The Cambridge Police Department also remembers all its officers—past and present—who serve the people of Cambridge with distinction.

This granite memorial, located in the Cambridge Cemetery, was erected by the Cambridge Police Mutual Aid Association in 1960. The inscription reads, "In memory of departed members of the Cambridge Police Department who have served the people of this city with honor and valor."

www.ingramcontent.com/pod-product-compliance
Lightning Source LLC
LaVergne TN
LVHW081531100826
845153LV00004B/254

* 9 7 8 1 5 3 1 6 4 0 2 9 3 *